DIVINE DWELLING

LIVING IN THE SECRET PLACE

A Devotional Exposition
Of Psalm 91

Patricia L. Hulsey

ISBN 978-1-930703-29-2

Printed in the USA by
Harvestime International Network
http://www.harvestime.org

TABLE OF CONTENTS

Introduction

When you were a child, did you have a secret hiding place-- somewhere you went to be alone, where you felt safe and secure? Perhaps it was a tree house or a window seat in your home. Maybe it was a dusty attic or a cozy basement. If you lived in a remote village, perhaps you had a special place under a certain tree, by a stream of water, or in a cleft in the mountain. You went to your secret place when you were upset, fearful, sad, or when you needed to retreat to a quiet, secure place.

Psalm 91 of the Holy Bible describes a spiritual hiding place located under the shadow of Almighty God where you can be safe and secure no matter what circumstances you are experiencing in your life, your home, your ministry, on the job, or in your nation. It is a spiritual place that all believers can access, a secure habitation where you can abide continually.

The United States has tornado, bomb, and earthquake shelters in various parts of the nation to provide places of safety for people in times of crisis. But the spiritual dwelling of which you will learn in this study is a place where you can abide continually. You don't have to flee there in times of crisis, because you are already there!

Psalm 91 is a message to those who have or who will face challenges, problems, and difficult circumstances. In other words, it is a Psalm for everyone, but there are specific qualifications in order to claim its promises. The promises of Psalm 91 are for those who abide in the secret place. When you experience crisis outside of this spiritual dwelling, you cannot claim the provisions, protection, and promises of this passage. That is why it is important to learn how to gain access to the secret place and remain there permanently.

First and foremost, in order to dwell in this secret place you must abide in the shadow of Almighty God, which by implication requires that you must be a follower of the one and only God whose Son is Jesus Christ. If you are not already a born-again believer, here are the steps to take:

Recognize you are a sinner: *For all have sinned, and come short of the glory of God. (Romans 3:23)*

Understand that the penalty of sin is death: *For the wages of sin is death; but the gift of God is eternal life through Jesus Christ our Lord. (Romans 6:23)*

Realize that God loves you and gave His Son to die for your sins: *But God commendeth his love toward us, in that, while we were yet sinners, Christ died for us. (Romans 5:8)*

Understand that there is nothing you can do to earn your salvation: *For by grace are ye saved through faith; and that not of yourselves: it is the gift of God: Not of works, lest any man should boast. (Ephesians 2:8-9)*

Acknowledge that there is only one way to salvation: *Neither is there salvation in any other: for there is none other name under heaven given among men, whereby we must be saved. (Acts 4:12)*

Ask God to forgive your sins: *If we say that we have no sin, we deceive ourselves, and the truth is not in us. If we confess our sins, he is faithful and just to forgive us our sins, and to cleanse us from all unrighteousness. (1 John 1:8-9)*

Confess and believe that Jesus is Lord and that God raised Him from the dead: *But what saith it? The word is nigh thee, even in thy mouth, and in thy heart: that is, the word of faith, which we preach; That if thou shalt confess with thy mouth the Lord Jesus, and shalt believe in thine heart that God hath raised him from the dead, thou shalt be saved. For with the heart man believeth unto righteousness; and with the mouth confession is made unto salvation. (Romans 10:8-10)*

The promises of Psalm 91 are conditional, meaning there are certain requirements that must be met in order to claim them. It is much like the guarantee on a product you purchase. There are certain requirements that must be met in order for the guarantee to be valid.

As a born-again believer in Jesus Christ, you have already met the first and most important requirement. If you are a true believer--even if you just became one as you followed the directives in this introductory section--you are ready to receive the revelations of Psalm 91.

In the natural world, you may live in a shack, a crowded housing project, a middle class neighborhood, or a mansion-- no matter. You are invited to come on in to the secret place!

Welcome home!

The Appendix of this book features twenty-one different versions of Psalm 91 so you can read the passage in a different translation prior to commencing each chapter in this study.

SECTION ONE
DIVINE PRESENCE

"He who dwells in the secret place
of the Most High
Shall abide under the shadow of the Almighty.

I will say of the Lord,
'He is my refuge and my fortress;
My God, in Him I will trust.'"

(Psalm 91:1-2)

Chapter One
Dwelling In The Secret Place

"He who dwells in the secret place of the Most High..."

A covenant, as used in the Bible, is a relationship based upon mutual commitments between two or more people involving promises and obligations on behalf of each party.

The Bible records seven major covenants between God and mankind. These include the Adamic, Abramaic, Noahic, Palestinian, Mosaic, Davidic, and the New Covenant. Some of these are unconditional, meaning they will be fulfilled regardless of what man does. Others, like the Old Testament Mosaic Covenant, are conditional, meaning it requires obedience in order to receive the promises. (Deuteronomy 28-29).

Psalm 91 is not identified by theologians as a major covenant, but it certainly has the qualities of a covenant because the promises are conditional. That is why, in the introduction to this study, we covered the first requirement for qualifying for the blessings of Psalm 91--that of becoming a true follower of God.

Psalm 91 can only be understood by a spiritual mind that has been regenerated by the new birth experience because *"...the natural man receiveth not the things of the Spirit of God: for they are foolishness unto him: neither can he know them, because they are spiritually discerned" (1 Corinthians 2:14).*

In the first part of verse one of Psalm 91 we find a major key for claiming the promises of this amazing passage: You must dwell in the secret place of the Most High.

11

He who dwells in the secret place of the Most High shall remain stable and fixed under the shadow of the Almighty [Whose power no foe can withstand]. (Psalm 91:1, AMP)

Here are some other versions of this verse:

-The one who lives under the protection of the Most High dwells in the shadow of the Almighty. (Holman)

-Whoever dwells in the shelter of the Most High will rest in the shadow of the Almighty. (NIRV)

-He that dwelleth in the help of the highest God; shall dwell in the protection of God of heaven. (He who dwelleth in the shelter of the Most High God, shall live under the protection of the God of heaven.) (Wycliff)

The remainder of Psalm 91 are promises for those who consistently dwell in the secret place of the Most High. So this passage raises several questions:

-Who is the Most High?
-Where is the secret place?
-What does it mean to dwell in the secret place?

We must discover the answers to these questions before we can claim the promises of this beautiful passage.

The Most High

In Genesis 14:18-20, God revealed Himself to Abraham as the Most High God, *"the possessor of heaven and earth"*. This is the first recorded revelation of God by this name.

Note that He is *the* Most High God--not *a* God or one among many. Note also that He possesses everything in heaven and in earth. He is the Most High God over all.

The Psalmist recognized this and admonished..."*That men may know that thou, whose name alone is Jehovah, art the most high over all the earth" (Psalm 83:18).*

Note the phrase *"whose name alone is Jehovah"*. When we speak of the Most High God, we are talking about the one true God. Even Satan acknowledged the Most High God when he aspired to usurp His position (Isaiah 14:14) and demons proclaimed Jesus as the Son of the Most High God (Luke 8:28).

So the Most High God spoken of in Psalm 91:1 is the one and only true God as revealed in the Old and New Testaments of the Holy Bible.

The Secret Place

Having determined who is "the Most High", let us address the next question: Where is the secret place?

The secret place referred to in this verse is not the final resting place of some man who claimed he was god and is now dead. It is not the dwelling place of some idol or the headquarters of a person who claims deity. It is the secret place of the one true and living Most High God in which believers must consistently dwell in order to claim the promises of this chapter.

The secret place is not a doctrinal position or an actual physical location. It is not a cathedral or monastery, no matter how beautiful the buildings may be, because *"...the most High dwelleth not in temples made with hands" (Acts 7:48).*

The "*secret place*" described in this Psalm is an intimate place of personal relationship with God. It can be compared to the holy of holies in the Old Testament tabernacle. Masses of God's people assembled in the outer court to worship God, but only a chosen few accessed the holy of holies and entered the presence of the Most High God.

After the death of Jesus Christ on the cross for the sin of all mankind, the veil which concealed the holy of holies was torn apart: *"And, behold, the veil of the temple was rent in twain from the top to the bottom..." (Matthew 27:51).* This supernatural event was symbolic of the new, unprecedented access to God which was opened through the sacrificial death of Jesus Christ:

> *Having therefore, brethren, boldness to enter into the holiest by the blood of Jesus, By a new and living way, which he hath consecrated for us, through the veil, that is to say, his flesh; And having an high priest over the house of God; Let us draw near with a true heart in full assurance of faith, having our hearts sprinkled from an evil conscience, and our bodies washed with pure water. (Hebrews 10:19-22)*

Because of Jesus, the way is open for you to be cleansed from sin and enter into the secret place of God's presence, a spiritual habitation of personal intimacy with the Most High God. The way is open to all believers, but you must choose to dwell there. You can be as close as you choose to be because Jesus secured your access through His death on the cross.

Dwelling In The Secret Place

Many people go through life asking God for a blessing here and there, or calling for help in times of crisis. But Psalm 91 reveals that there is an intimate, secret place of relationship with God where you can dwell permanently and continually experience His supernatural provision and protection.

Young's Literal Translation renders this verse as *"He who is dwelling, In the secret place of the Most High, In the shade of the Mighty lodgeth habitually."* Other versions of this verse indicate that those who dwell in the secret place are under the defense of the Most High, under His protection, and living as His ward.

Dwelling in the secret place conveys the idea of being at home with God. Analogies can be drawn between this and the physical home where you live. Your home is a storehouse of all you need--clothing, equipment, food, supplies etc. In the secret place with God, you have all you need spiritually, as Psalm 91 reflects.

In your physical home, you have a bedroom for rest. God provides rest for your soul in the secret place. Jesus said, *"Come unto me, all ye that labour and are heavy laden, and I will give you rest. Take my yoke upon you, and learn of me; for I am meek and lowly in heart: and ye shall find rest unto your souls" (Matthew 11:28-29).*

In your home there is an area set apart for preparing and eating food. In the secret place you receive spiritual nutrition from God's Word. Your home also has a bathroom where you cleanse yourself and a toilet where you dispose of waste. Likewise, the secret place is where you are spiritually cleansed and eliminate the wastes of the world. Your home has a living room where you fellowship with family and friends. Your secret place is where you can fellowship with God and be at home spiritually.

It is in the secret place--dwelling with God consistently--that hidden spiritual riches are bestowed:

> *And I will give thee the treasures of darkness, and hidden riches of secret places, that thou mayest know that I, the Lord, which call thee by thy name, am the God of Israel. (Isaiah 45:3)*

Some of those "hidden riches" of the secret place include wisdom to guide your life and ministry properly and knowledge to bless and help others. The secrets of effective prayer and the mysteries of God's Word are also revealed in the secret place.

The secret place is a position of total intimacy, a place where you commune constantly with the Lord--and that can happen in a closet, in the car, in the living room, sitting in your garden--anywhere. The place is not important because the secret place is not a physical location.

Have you accessed this spiritual secret place? Do you have an intimate personal relationship with God? This is the prerequisite for possessing the promises of Psalm 91. The covenant discussed in this Psalm is only for those who dwell in the secret place under the shadow of the Almighty.

Many of us run to God in times of crisis, but we do not habitually reside in Him. When things get better, we go back to doing our own thing. We sometimes treat God like a motel: We check in when we need Him and check out when we think we no longer have a need.

There is a difference between dwelling somewhere and just dropping in from time-to-time. You drop by for a visit at the home of a friend or family member, but you dwell permanently in your own house. God doesn't want you to just drop in to visit during times of trouble. He wants you to habitually dwell in the secret place--to live there, settle down, and remain in residence there spiritually.

It becomes obvious that in order to dwell in this secret place, you must make time to be alone with God. Just as an intimate relationship between a man and his wife develops through time in seclusion, so does the intimate relationship between God and His spiritual bride--the Church. Intimacy is fostered by time spent together in the seclusion of your secret place. It is there you get to know Him. It is there that spiritual conception occurs and new dreams and visions are birthed.

When you learn to dwell habitually in the secret place, you will then understand what it means to abide in God. No longer will you be up and down in your Christian experience. No longer will you waffle between the Church and the world. You will learn how to abide permanently in Him--which brings us to the second part of Psalm 91:1 and the next portion of this study: Learning how to abide under the shadow of the Almighty.

Chapter Two
Abiding Under The Shadow

"...shall abide under the
shadow of the Almighty."

The second portion of Psalm 91:1 yields additional insight to understanding the secret place. This divine dwelling--this spiritual retreat, so to speak--is located under the shadow of Almighty God and it is there you are to abide:

> *He who dwells in the secret place of the Most High shall remain stable and fixed under the shadow of the Almighty [Whose power no foe can withstand].*
> *(Psalm 91:1, AMP)*

Other versions refer to the shadow of the Almighty as a shelter, shade, protection, and a place where one should lodge habitually. The word "abide" as used in the Bible means to "continue with, cling to, cleave to, and remain with"--all implying permanence.

This passage raises several questions:

-What does it mean to abide in God?
-What should you do if you fail to abide in Him?
-What is the shadow of the Almighty?
-Who is the Almighty God?
-How can you live continually in His presence?

Abiding In God

In this modern era we stay connected with those we love through personal contact, cell phones, texting, the Internet, and social networking sites. Intimacy develops from staying connected. To develop intimacy with God, we must also stay connected. We must learn to abide in His shadow. John chapter 15 uses the natural example of a vine and its branches to illustrate this concept of staying connected to God:

> *I am the true vine, and my Father is the husbandman...Abide in me, and I in you. As the branch cannot bear fruit of itself, except it abide in the vine; no more can ye, except ye abide in me. I am the vine, ye are the branches: He that abideth in me, and I in him, the same bringeth forth much fruit: for without me ye can do nothing. If a man abide not in me, he is cast forth as a branch, and is withered; and men gather them, and cast them into the fire, and they are burned. If ye abide in me, and my words abide in you, ye shall ask what ye will, and it shall be done unto you. (Portions of John 15:1-7)*

In this analogy, Jesus is the vine and true believers are the branches. A branch that is cut off from the vine does not last long and definitely does not bring forth fruit. You must stay connected to Jesus as branches are to a vine in order for supernatural life to continue to flow into you and produce spiritual growth.

This spiritual intimacy with God is a closer tie than those of kinship, for Jesus said, *"...whosoever shall do the will of God, the same is my brother, and my sister, and mother" (Mark 3:35)*. When you abide with someone long enough, you come to know their voice, their likes and dislikes, and their secrets. In other words, you come to know their heart.

Abiding in God's shadow means that a person has accepted Jesus Christ as Savior and is allowing the Word of God to abide in his life (1 John 2:24). It means experiencing the indwelling of the Holy Spirit (1 John 4:13) and having power to live a holy life (Ephesians 1:4). When you are abiding in God, you will live a fruitful life (John 15:5) and love others (1 John 4:11-12). You will not continue in deliberate sin (1 John 3:6) and you will endeavor to do God's will (1 John 2:17).

Abiding is necessary for a productive prayer life. Jesus promised:

> *If ye abide in me, and my words abide in you, ye shall ask what ye will, and it shall be done unto you. (John 15:7)*

This intimate relationship of abiding involves you abiding in Him and His Word abiding in you. The result is that you can ask what you will, and it shall be done!

This intimate relationship of abiding with God is best modeled by the Psalmist David, *"... to whom also he (God) gave testimony, and said, I have found David the son of Jesse, a man after mine own heart, which shall fulfil all my will"* (Acts 13:22). Many people only know David in regards to his sin with Bathsheba which, in western nations, has been popularized by movies. Others know David from Sunday school lessons as the shepherd boy who killed the giant Goliath and later became a king. But David was much more than that. He is the only man in Scripture called a man after God's own heart. He was one of whom it was declared that he fulfilled God's purposes in his generation, meaning that he achieved his spiritual destiny (Acts 13:36).

21

What does it mean to be a man after God's heart? It does not mean perfection, because David was not perfect. It is not based on education, because David was a simple shepherd boy at the time of his anointing as king. It was not because David came from the ideal family, because he did not. His brothers were judgmental, angry, and suspicious (1 Samuel 17:28). His father didn't even think enough of David to call him in from the field when the Prophet Samuel came to visit (1 Samuel 16:11-12).

To be a person after God's own heart means to be God's kindred spirit, someone to His liking, one in whom God finds a special affinity and delight. It is a person who, when confronted with sin, quickly humbles himself and confesses it and forgives others with the same forgiveness he has received from God. Such a person has a heart that is grieved by things that grieve the heart of God. They have the heart of a worshiper and continually abide in the presence of the Lord, as David did. Many of the songs in the Psalms were written in solitude with God. A person after God's heart doesn't just "put in their time" with the Lord. They cherish and relish time spent in His presence.

Failure To Abide

In Revelation 2:1-7, the Apostle John was directed by the Holy Spirit to pen a message to the church at Ephesus, a congregation that had left their first love and abandoned their intimacy with God:

> *Unto the angel of the church of Ephesus write; These things saith he that holdeth the seven stars in his right hand, who walketh in the midst of the seven golden candlesticks; I know thy works, and thy labour, and thy patience, and how thou canst not bear them which*

are evil: and thou hast tried them which say they are apostles, and are not, and hast found them liars: And hast borne, and hast patience, and for my name's sake hast laboured, and hast not fainted. Nevertheless I have somewhat against thee, because thou hast left thy first love. Remember therefore from whence thou art fallen, and repent, and do the first works; or else I will come unto thee quickly, and will remove thy candlestick out of his place, except thou repent. But this thou hast, that thou hatest the deeds of the Nicolaitans, which I also hate. He that hath an ear, let him hear what the Spirit saith unto the churches; To him that overcometh will I give to eat of the tree of life, which is in the midst of the paradise of God. (Revelation 2:1-7)

The church at Ephesus was over forty years old when John wrote this message. A new generation of believers had arisen who did not have the same fervency of love and devotion as those who received the Gospel when the Church was first established. The Ephesian believers had performed many good works, persevered patiently, endured hardship, and exhibited discernment in identifying false teachers. But-- tragically--they had abandoned their first love.

Like the believers at Ephesus, many of us are part of a large congregation of professing believers, we attend great cathedrals, and we minister in big organizations and denominations. But like the Ephesians, some of us have left our first love. We have replaced our love for God with our work for God and we no longer enjoy the intimacy of the secret place in His presence.

Jesus acknowledged, *"I know thy works",* but then He said, *"I have somewhat against thee, because thou has left thy first love" (Revelation 2:4).* Jesus did not say the Ephesian believers had forgotten their first love or that they had lost it, but that they had left it. The Greek word used for "left" is *aphiemi*, which means "to forsake." Believers had lost the fervency and intensity of their first love for God. They continued doing good works, but their deeds were no longer motivated and fueled by love. They were caught up in a routine of doing good things which became "dead works" without the passion and presence of God. These believers had forsaken the intimacy of the secret place.

Jesus warned the church at Ephesus to "*repent, and do the first works*". The first works to which the Ephesus church was admonished to return can be compared with the first love of a new marriage. A new bride is so in love with her husband that he is the central focus of her life. When she takes her wedding vows, she promises to forsake all others and give herself solely to him. She eagerly anticipates his desires and lovingly tries to meet his needs. She spends every possible moment with him.

Fervent spiritual love will motivate you to do whatever is necessary in order to be able to have time alone with your beloved Heavenly Father. You will look forward to daily communion with Him where you can pour out your heart and allow Him to speak to you. Your spiritual relationship with the Lord will be closer than any natural bond:

> *Anyone who loves his father or mother more than me is not worthy of me; anyone who loves his son or daughter more than me is not worthy of me; and anyone who does not take his cross and follow me is not worthy of me. Whoever finds his life will lose it, and whoever loses his life for my sake will find it. (Matthew 10:37-39, NIV)*

In this bridal-love relationship, there is a special intimacy that develops between the bride and her bridegroom. She longs to know everything possible about him. She opens her heart to him, revealing her innermost secrets and desires. When they are apart from one another, she longs for him and eagerly anticipates when she will be with him again. Because of her love, the bride puts her bridegroom first before all else, including her own needs, desires, and ambitions. And in the intimacy of the secret place, they conceive new life.

It is in the secret place with God that this type of pure, fervent, bridal love is nurtured spiritually. Just as Jesus called the church in Ephesus to return to their first love, He is walking among us today, calling us--as the Bride of Christ--to repent and return to our first love, to come on back to the secret place. Here are six warning signs that you have abandoned the secret place and your passionate first love for God has faded:

1. When Christ is no longer the central focus of your life. When other desires, people, activities, and things take preeminence, it is an indication that you have left your first love.

2. When you neglect your relationship with God and spend less time in prayer, worship, and the Word. There are many believers--including pastors and leaders--who are so busy in the work of the Lord that they neglect spending time alone with God, seeking and worshiping Him, and allowing Him to speak to them.

3. When there is a loss of intimacy in your relationship with God. You find it difficult to hear God speak to you because you haven't spent time in His presence. When you abide in the secret place, you come to know His voice.

4. When you are caught in a cycle of dead works. Your work for God becomes a drudgery or business-like. Instead of being motivated by love, it becomes a duty, form, or ritual.

5. When you become tolerant of sin. The true test of love for the Lord is obedience. John wrote, *"For this is the love of God, that we keep his commandments: and his commandments are not grievous" (1 John 5:3)*. Jesus said, *"If ye love me, keep my commandments" (John 14:15)*.

6. When you no longer have a burning passion for the lost. It was their strong fervent love for Christ that motivated members of the early church to share the Gospel everywhere they went. Their great love for lost souls was manifested to the extent that they were willing to lay down their lives in order to bring souls into the Kingdom of God.

Take time right now to examine your relationship with the Lord. Are any of these major indicators present? Reflect back on when you first came to know the Lord and your love for Him burned fervently with unbridled passion. Your works then were motivated by an intense love and devotion to the Lord. Compare your love for God today with what it was then. Has your love grown deeper or has it lost its fervency? Are your current works motivated by a passionate love for God or are you doing them merely out of a sense of duty?

If you have left your first love and abandoned the secret place, do what Jesus commanded and *"remember therefore from whence thou art fallen and repent, and do the first works..." (Revelation 2:5)*. Ask the Lord to forgive you for leaving your first love. Begin to do your first works again. Make a new commitment to the basics of prayer, worship, and the Word. Fan the flame of the dying embers of your first love through renewed communion with the Lord.

Abiding Under The Shadow

To be under the shadow of another, you must be close to them. You must follow them or walk alongside of them, not rush ahead or lag too far behind. You cannot be in the shadow of someone unless you are traveling the same direction along the same path. The minute you take a different turn in the road from your companion, you will no longer be in their shadow.

The Bible reveals that you will walk in the shadow of someone, whether they be good or evil. God warns about walking in the shadow of Egypt, which is symbolic of the world. The Word commands, *"...trust not in the shadow of Egypt"* *(Isaiah 30:2)* and notes that those who walk in the shadow of Egypt (in sinful ways and with sinful people) will have nothing but confusion (Isaiah 30:3). The Bible also speaks of the shadow of darkness, again referring to sin, but proclaiming the good news that *"The people which sat in darkness saw great light; and to them which sat in the region and shadow of death light is sprung up"* *(Matthew 4:16)*. Are you walking in the shadow of sin, or abiding in the shadow of Almighty God?

To walk in God's shadow you must choose to go His way, which begins with the decision you made when you became a believer. After your conversion to Christ, you must learn to walk with God consistently through regular prayer, worship, and study of the Word. David said, *"Thy word is a lamp unto my feet, and a light unto my path"* *(Psalm 119:105)* and *"I will run in the way of thy commandments"* *(Psalm 119:32)*. He prayed, *"Teach me thy way, O Lord, and lead me in a plain path..."* *(Psalm 27:11)*. Proverbs 4:26-27 encourages us to *"Ponder the path of thy feet, and let all thy ways be established. Turn not to the right hand nor to the left: remove thy foot from evil."*

You can't rush ahead or fall too far behind God, or you will lose His shadow. You must move when He moves and stop when He stops. Each day, you must make the choice to remain in His shadow instead of doing your own thing. The Apostle John declared, *"He that abideth in him ought himself also to walk, even as he walked"* (1 John 2:6).

There is an Old Testament example that aptly illustrates this concept. When the children of Israel left the bondage of Egypt--symbolizing the world--to travel to their promised land, they advanced or stopped according to the movement of a supernatural cloud:

> *And when the cloud was taken up from over the tabernacle, the children of Israel went onward in all their journeys: But if the cloud were not taken up, then they journeyed not till the day that it was taken up. For the cloud of the Lord was upon the tabernacle by day, and fire was on it by night, in the sight of all the house of Israel, throughout all their journeys. (Exodus 40:36-38)*

As long as the people remained under that cloud, they had the protection of its shadow by day (cooling) and its fire by night (heat). Under the cloud, they received daily manna because that was the place of provision (Numbers 9). The same is true regarding the shadow of the Almighty. When you are walking God's way, you are in His shadow. You remain there by choice. You make a daily decision to abide in the place of provision and protection.

The Prophet Isaiah declared regarding God's shadow, *"For thou hast been a strength to the poor, a strength to the needy in his distress, a refuge from the storm, a shadow from the heat"* (Isaiah 25:4).

The bride in the Song of Solomon, symbolic of the bride of Christ, declared: *"As the apple tree among the trees of the wood, so is my beloved among the sons. I sat down under his shadow with great delight, and his fruit was sweet to my taste" (Song of Solomon 2:3).*

Living in the shadow of God is where you find protection, provision, direction, and intimacy. It is where you are refreshed and renewed and where you experience great delight.

The Almighty God

Psalm 91:1 declares that if you dwell in the secret place of the Most High, you will abide under the shadow of the Almighty. We have defined the meaning of dwelling and abiding and discussed what it means to be under the shadow. So who is the Almighty to whom this passage refers?

In the first portion of Psalm 91:1, God is referred to as the Most High. Here we encounter another name for God: The Almighty. In Genesis 17:1, God first revealed Himself as the Almighty to Abraham declaring, *"...I am the Almighty God."* Again, note that He is *the* Almighty God, not *a* god. There is only one Almighty God, and it is the same "Most High" of whom we studied in the previous portion of this verse.

"Almighty God" means the all-sufficient God. It comes from the Hebrew word *"shaadah"* which means "to pour out." In essence, God was telling Abraham, "I am the one and only true God who pours out blessings richly, abundantly, and continually."

"Almighty God" is one of the first names of God revealed in Genesis, and the last by which God refers to Himself in Revelation 1:8 where He declares, *"I am Alpha and Omega, the beginning and the ending, saith the Lord, which is, and which was, and which is to come, the Almighty."* This name is also used when God describes His relationship with you as your Heavenly Father (2 Corinthians 6:18).

When you dwell in the secret place and abide under the shadow of the Almighty, you are placing yourself under the care of an all-sufficient, all powerful God who will continually pour His abundant riches and blessings into your life. You can certainly dwell securely in the hands of such a God.

Abiding In God's Presence

In Psalm chapter 15, the meanings of "dwelling" and "abiding" about which you have been studying in Psalm 91 are expanded. Five short verses provide practical guidelines for living in the presence of the Lord.

> *Lord, who shall abide in thy tabernacle? Who shall dwell in thy holy hill? He that walketh uprightly, and worketh righteousness, and speaketh the truth in his heart. He that backbiteth not with his tongue, nor doeth evil to his neighbour, nor taketh up a reproach against his neighbour. In whose eyes a vile person is contemned; but he honoureth them that fear the Lord. He that sweareth to his own hurt, and changeth not. He that putteth not out his money to usury, nor taketh reward against the innocent. He that doeth these things shall never be moved. (Psalm 15:1-5)*

First, this psalm begins with crucial questions that every person must answer. Second, it gives key principles that enable believers to abide continually in God's presence. Third, the passage ends with an amazing promise to those who put these principles into practice.

The author of this psalm was David. On the surface you would think that God would have chosen anybody but David to share this message. His life was a roller-coaster ride of challenges--from facing Goliath victoriously to falling into great sin, from enduring a king's wrath to becoming king himself and having a son try to overthrow his kingdom and kill him. On the outside, David's life was a model of turbulence rather than stability. Yet, in his heart of hearts, he was totally committed to God. He was called, "a man after God's own heart" because he dwelt continually in the secret place with God.

The psalmist begins Psalm 15 with two questions: *"Who shall **abide** in Thy tabernacle? Who shall **dwell** in Thy holy hill?"* The fact that David raises these questions shows that we are not entitled to dwell in God's presence as a right of natural birth or bloodline.

The word "tabernacle" speaks of a temporary dwelling. Other versions use the word "tent" in this verse, so a composite translation might read, "Lord, who can pitch his tent and dwell with You, day-by-day, here on earth? Who has the right to enter Your tent?"

The "holy hill" referred to in this passage speaks of permanence. Hebrew scholars knew that the holy hill of Mount Zion referred to God's heavenly kingdom, so the second question carries with it the idea, "Lord, who can dwell with You in heaven as well?"

So the psalmist is asking, "Who can abide with you temporarily in the day-to-day walk of life, while we--like Israel--are pilgrims. And then, who can abide with You permanently for all eternity?" In Hebrew, these questions are rhetorical, meaning that the writer assumes you know the answers. If you do not know the answer to these questions, you can know--and that is one purpose for this study!

The one who can dwell with God continually on earth and for eternity in heaven is someone who has made a personal commitment to Jesus Christ, who has not only asked Him to forgive their sins, but also to be the Lord of their life. Psalm 15 provides practical guidelines to allow the Lord to govern your life in five major areas: Your testimony, your tongue, your thoughts, your trustworthiness, and your treasure.

Your testimony. Psalm 15:2 indicates that *"He that walks uprightly, and works righteousness, and speaks the truth in his heart"* will gain access to God's dwelling place.

"Walking uprightly" means to walk with integrity, "to be sound, complete, without crack or defect." Believers are to have an identical public and private self. They are to be people who refuse to compromise or cut ethical corners. What you do when no one is looking reflects the true level of your integrity.

"Working righteousness" carries the idea of doing what is proper even when it is difficult. This not only means to abstain from sin, but to do what is right because *"..to him that knoweth to do good, and doeth it not, to him it is sin" (James 4:17).*

"Speaking the truth in your heart" refers to your innermost thoughts. Whether or not you speak the truth in your heart will be reflected in your work and your walk. The Bible says, *"For as a man thinks in his heart, so is he" (Proverbs 23:7).* What you think affects your conduct, and that, of course, affects your testimony. Jesus said, *"...for out of the abundance of the heart the mouth speaketh. A good man out of the good treasure of the heart bringeth forth good things: and an evil* man out of the evil treasure bringeth forth evil things" (Matthew 12:34-35).

What truth are you are to embrace in your heart that will be reflected in your testimony? It is the truth of God's Word. The Bible declares, "...thy Word is truth" (John 17:17).

Your tongue. Next, the psalmist declares that the one who wishes to gain access to God's presence "backbiteth not with his tongue, nor doeth evil to his neighbour, nor taketh up a reproach against his neighbour" (Psalm 15:3). Three things related to your tongue are addressed in this verse: Accountability, actions, and attitudes.

> -Accountability: In Hebrew, what is pictured by the word "backbiting" is the deliberate act of picking up something destructive and placing it on your tongue. You are accountable for your words.

> -Actions: You don't have to do something drastic to sin against a person--just damage their reputation, treat them badly, or spoil something good that should have come their way.

> -Attitudes: Do not harbor reproach, bitterness, or unforgiveness in your relationships.

A related passage in Psalm 24 addresses these areas of accountability, actions, and attitudes in similar terms. The Psalmist asks "Who shall ascend into the hill of the Lord? or who shall stand in his holy place?" Then he answers, "He that hath clean hands, and a pure heart; who hath not lifted up his soul unto vanity, nor sworn deceitfully" (Psalm 24:3-4).

Your thoughts. Verse 4 addresses your thinking, stating: "*In whose eyes a vile person is despised, but he honors those who fear the Lord...*" You are to despise those who are vile and honor those worthy of honor. Respect should be given those whose lives reflect godly conduct and commitments. Conversely, sports stars, entertainment celebrities, or business figures who may light up the scoreboard, the big screen, or win corporate awards but have godless characters are to be counted as worthless. Who are your heroes? Who are you modeling your life after? Who you honor reflects your values, and your values affect whether or not you will dwell in the secret place of intimate fellowship with God.

Your trustworthiness. The man or woman of God who "*swears to his own hurt, and does not change*" is the one who will dwell in God's presence (verse 4). Another version says, "*He keeps his word and does not change*" A person who is trustworthy doesn't cut corners on a contract or explain away an obligation. He doesn't commit to do something and then not show up. He is trustworthy, meaning he is worthy of trust.

When you commit to do something and do not follow through, there are two major negative results. First, you create a barrier between you and God because according to this Psalm you must be a person who keeps his word in order to dwell with Him. It doesn't mean you lose your salvation, but when you do not keep your word you are straying from His shadow and that is when you get into difficulties. Second, you nullify the power of your spiritual confessions. Confession is basic to your salvation, healing, deliverance, etc. There is tremendous spiritual power in confession. Satan listens to the words that come out of your mouth. If you commit to do something and then don't follow through, he concludes that obviously you don't mean what you say so why should he take your spiritual confessions seriously?

Your treasure. The final portion of Psalm 15:5 addresses the use of your material resources stating, *"He who does not put out his money at usury, nor does he take a bribe against the innocent."* An intimate relationship with God involves financial integrity. You are not to lend money at unlawful rates, charge interest greater than the principal, or require payment rates that you know a borrower is unable to make. (This does not mean you cannot earn interest through commercial banks or business investments.) You are also cautioned not to take a reward against the innocent, meaning to neither give or receive a bribe to pervert justice or injure an innocent man.

You Will Never Be Moved

Psalm 15 closes with the assurance that *"...he that does these things shall never be moved" (verse 5).* He who does what things? The things discussed in this chapter. The one who:
> -Walks uprightly.
> -Works righteousness.
> -Speaks the truth in his heart.
> -Controls his tongue.
> -Does no evil.
> -Does not take up a reproach against his neighbor.
> -Views a vile person with contempt.
> -Honors those who fear the Lord.
> -Swears to his own hurt and does not change.
> -Is fair and honest in his financial dealings.

He who does these things will never be moved from where? He will never be moved from his place of dwelling in the secret place with God.

Other versions of Psalm 15:5 declare: *"He who does these things will never fail...never be overthrown...nothing can ever shake him...never be brought low...he who so lives will stand firm forever!"*

In most guarantees, there are disclaimers, perhaps phrases like these: "Some exclusions apply. May not be valid in all locations. Your results may not be the same as King David's!" But there are no disclaimers here because this psalm is backed by Almighty God Who promises you a place in His presence where you will never be moved when you live by these guidelines.

In closing this chapter, meditate on Psalm 15 in various translations of the Bible to further expand your understanding of the biblical guidelines for dwelling in the secret place.

The Living Bible
Lord, who may go and find refuge and shelter in your tabernacle up on your holy hill? Anyone who leads a blameless life and is truly sincere. Anyone who refuses to slander others, does not listen to gossip, never harms his neighbor, speaks out against sin, criticizes those committing it, commends the faithful followers of the Lord, keeps a promise even if it ruins him, does not crush his debtors with high interest rates, and refuses to testify against the innocent despite the bribes offered him: Such a man shall stand firm forever.

The New American Standard Version
O Lord, who may abide in Thy tent? Who may dwell on Thy holy hill? He who walks with integrity, and works righteousness, and speaks truth in his heart. He does not slander with his tongue, nor does evil to his neighbor, nor takes up a reproach against his friend; In whose eyes a reprobate is despised, but who honors those who fear the Lord; He swears to his own hurt, and does not change; He does not put out his money at interest, nor does he take a

bribe against the innocent. He who does these things will never be shaken.

The New International Version
Lord, who may dwell in your sanctuary? Who may live on your holy hill? He whose walk is blameless and who does what is righteous, who speaks the truth from his heart and has no slander on his tongue, who does his neighbor no wrong and casts no slur on his fellow man, who despises a vile man but honors those who fear the Lord, who keeps his oath even when it hurts, who lends his money without usury and does not accept a bribe against the innocent. He who does these things will never be shaken.

The Amplified Bible
Lord, who shall dwell [temporarily] in Your tabernacle? Who shall dwell [permanently] on Your holy hill? He who walks and lives uprightly and blamelessly, who works rightness and justice and speaks and thinks the truth in his heart, He who does not slander with his tongue, nor does evil to his friend, nor takes up a reproach against his neighbor. In whose eyes a vile person is despised, but he who honors those who fear the Lord (who revere and worship Him; who swears to his own hurt and does not change; [He who] does not put out his money for interest to one of his own people and who will not take a bribe against the innocent. He who does these things shall never be moved.

Chapter Three
Confessing The Lord

"I will say of the Lord,
He is my refuge and my fortress,
my God..."

In Psalm 91:2, the psalmist declares: *"I will say to the Lord, 'You are my place of safety and protection. You are my God and I trust you'" (New Century Version).*

Other versions translate this verse as:

> *-He is saying of Jehovah, "My refuge, and my bulwark, my God, I trust in Him," (Youngs)*

> *-He shall say to the Lord, Thou art mine up-taker, and my refuge; my God, I shall hope in him. (He shall say to the Lord, Thou art my defender, and my refuge; my God, I trust in thee.) (Wycliff)*

> *-Whoever goes to the Lord for safety, whoever remains under the protection of the Almighty, can say to him, "You are my defender and protector. You are my God; in you I trust." (Good News)*

> *-I will say of the Lord, He is my Refuge and my Fortress, my God; on Him I lean and rely, and in Him I [confidently] trust! (AMP)*

> *-I will say about the Lord, "He is my place of safety. He is like a fort to me. He is my God. I trust in him." (NIV Readers)*

What powerful confessions! The various translations of this passage declare the Lord is a refuge, a place of safety and protection, a bulwark, an up-taker, a defender, like a fort, and one in whom you can confidently trust.

Romans 10:9 declares, *"If you confess with your mouth the Lord Jesus and believe in your heart that God has raised Him from the dead, you will be saved."* You are saved by believing in your heart and confessing with your mouth the truths of God's Word regarding Jesus Christ. You receive other spiritual benefits the same way, by believing and confessing God's Word. There is a definite relationship between confessing with your mouth and believing in your heart (Mark11:23). When your heart and your mouth are in agreement, supernatural power is released.

When you come to Jesus Christ as a sinner, the power of the new birth experience occurs when you ask forgiveness and confess Him as Savior. The Bible indicates you are to confess with your mouth, not just give mental ascent to the salvation process.

God works in your life on the basis of your confession. Did you notice that in churches that don't believe in divine healing and never confess the Lord as Healer, no one ever gets healed? If you never confess Jesus as your Savior, you won't be saved. If you never confess, "He is my Healer", you may not get healed!

Whatever you believe in your heart comes out in your confession (Luke 6:45). Whatever you believe and say of the Lord, that is what He will be in your life. Most believers confess that the Lord is their Savior, but He wants to be more than that to you. He wants to be your healer, your guide, your comforter, your deliverer, your provider, and your financier.

What Do You Say Of The Lord?

Proverbs 18:21 reveals that *"death and life are in the power of the tongue"*. So what do you say of the Lord? Are you making negative confessions? Are you blaming, accusing, and questioning God? Are you speaking death or life to your relationship with God? Others may curse God or accuse Him of being unjust--but what do you say of the Lord? What comes out of your mouth in times of trouble? Swear words? Angry words? Useless questions? Do you feel like following Mrs. Job's advice to "curse God and die"? (Job 2:9).

The person with an intimate relationship with God who is dwelling in the secret place and abiding under His shadow-- this is one who confesses, *"He is my refuge, my fortress, my God..."* Note that God is not just *a* refuge, but he is *my* refuge, *my* fortress, *my* God. This is a personal confession that arises from your own secret-place relationship with God. What your parents said about God is good, but it is not enough. What your preacher says about Him is good, but not enough. It is what *you* say about Him that releases the power of confession in your life.

Proper confession means you come into agreement with God and declare the same thing He has said in His Word: *"Let us hold fast the profession (confession) of our faith without wavering; for he is faithful that promised" (Hebrews 10:23).*

He Is My Refuge

The Psalmist declared, *"I will say of the Lord He is my refuge..." (Psalm 91:2).* The words "I will say" used here imply continuously saying something. A refuge speaks of a hiding place, a place of safety, security, and rest. When no one is there for you in times of trouble, when everyone fails you, God is your refuge. Don't look around for help. Look to Him.

The psalmist said *"...I looked on my right hand, and beheld, but there was no man that would know me: refuge failed me; no man cared for my soul. I cried unto thee, Oh Lord: I said, Thou art my refuge and my portion in the land of the living"* *(Psalms 142:4-5).* Throughout the Psalms, David repeatedly confirms that God is his refuge:

> *The Lord also will be a refuge for the oppressed, a refuge in times of trouble. (Psalms 9:9)*

> *God is our refuge and strength, a very present help in trouble. (Psalms 46:1)*

> *But I will sing of thy power; yea, I will sing aloud of thy mercy in the morning: for thou hast been my defence and refuge in the day of my trouble. (Psalms 59:16)*

> *In God is my salvation and my glory: the rock of my strength, and my refuge, is in God. (Psalms 62:7)*

In this sinful world, you will definitely need a refuge. Not just a vacation destination. Not just a day off once in awhile. You need a refuge where you can continually abide. The Prophet Isaiah declares:

> *For thou hast been a strength to the poor, a strength to the needy in his distress, a refuge from the storm, a shadow from the heat, when the blast of the terrible ones is as a storm against the wall. (Isaiah 25:4)*

Jeremiah calls God *"my refuge in the day of affliction"* *(Jeremiah 16:19)* and the Apostle Paul speaks of Him as a strong consolation to those who have fled to Him for refuge *(Hebrews 6:18).*

He Is My Fortress

The psalmist continues to say of the Lord, *"He is...my fortress..." (Psalm 91:2).* The Hebrew word "fortress" speaks of a watchtower where a guard is set, a place of fortification against an enemy.

The psalmist adds to the richness of this word when He declares that God is *"My goodness, and my fortress; my high tower, and my deliverer; my shield, and he in whom I trust; who subdueth my people under me" (Psalms 144:2).*

Because the Lord was His fortress, David was delivered from the power of the enemy:

> *The Lord is my rock, and my fortress, and my deliverer; my God, my strength, in whom I will trust; my buckler, and the horn of my salvation, and my high tower. (Psalm 18:2)*

David prayed. *"Be thou my strong habitation, whereunto I may continually resort: thou hast given commandment to save me; for thou art my rock and my fortress" (Psalm 71:3).*

The Prophet Jeremiah said of God, *"Oh Lord, my strength, and my fortress, and my refuge in the day of affliction..." (Jeremiah 16:19).*

Where do you flee in times of trouble? Who do you turn to? What is your response to affliction? Do you get angry because you don't understand the circumstances? Do you turn away from God or do you find shelter in your spiritual fortress?

If you are abiding in the secret place, you don't have to flee there because you are already there. He is your refuge and fortress because you are abiding in Him. You don't abandon Him in times of trouble, and He does not abandon you. You abide in His presence, secure in your secret place.

He Is My God

The final declaration the psalmist makes is that *"...He is my God!"*. This is the fourth in a series of names for God given in Psalm 91:1-2 that reflect increasing levels of intimacy. You have come to know God as Most High, Almighty, and the Lord Jehovah. Now you must come to know Him as *my* God.

You may understand that God is the one and only Most High God and that He is the Almighty, all powerful God. You may have heard of Him as Jehovah-God. But you must come to know Him as *"my God"*--He must become personal to you. This is more than intellectual or emotional knowledge, because even demons believe intellectually and respond emotionally by trembling, but they do not really know God (James 2:19).

There is a New Testament story in John 9 that illustrates various levels of knowing the Lord:

> *Now as Jesus passed by, He saw a man who was blind from birth. And His disciples asked Him, saying, "Rabbi, who sinned, this man or his parents, that he was born blind?" Jesus answered, "Neither this man nor his parents sinned, but that the works of God should be revealed in him. "I must work the works of Him who sent Me while it is day; the night is coming when no one can work. "As long as I am in the world, I am the light of the world." When He had said these*

things, He spat on the ground and made clay with the saliva; and He anointed the eyes of the blind man with the clay. And He said to him, "Go, wash in the pool of Siloam" (which is translated, Sent). So he went and washed, and came back seeing. (John 9:1-7)

Here was a man who was blind since birth until Jesus passed by and--in a rather unconventional way--healed him. Would you get in the prayer line today if you knew the minister was going to make mud with spit and put it on your eyes?

Carnal reasoning would say that this strange method would not make a blind man see, but Jesus was not bound by tradition. Jesus told the Pharisees that they erred spiritually because they were bound by tradition. Christ's approach was, "Don't just patch up the old by giving this man reading glasses or glass eyes that look good but still don't enable him to see. Give him new eyes!"

After his healing, this man was asked by friends and neighbors to explain how his eyes had been opened. The man answered, *"A Man called Jesus made clay and anointed my eyes and said to me, `Go to the pool of Siloam and wash.' So I went and washed, and I received sight."* Then the Pharisees questioned as to how the man received his sight, and he responded, *"He put clay on my eyes, and I washed, and I see...He is a prophet"* (Portions of John 9:15 and 17).

Next, unbelieving Jews questioned the formerly blind man. They did not believe Jesus was of God, but thought that He was a sinner. The blind man responded, "Whether he is a sinner or not I don't know, but one thing I know--I was blind, but now I see." The Jews were so angry at this response that they cast the man out of the synagogue. Then...

Jesus heard that they had cast him out; and when He had found him, He said to him, "Do you believe in the Son of God?" He answered and said, "Who is He, Lord, that I may believe in Him?" And Jesus said to him, "You have both seen Him and it is He who is talking with you." Then he said, "Lord, I believe!" And he worshiped Him. (John 9:35-38)

Note the progression in this man's relationship with the Lord as reflected in the answers he gave regarding his healing. In verse 11, he viewed Jesus as just a man. In verse 17, he calls Him a prophet. In verse 33, he realizes that Jesus is from God. Finally, in verse 38, the man acknowledges Jesus as Lord of his life and worships Him.

There is a difference between knowing Jesus as a man, a teacher, or a prophet and truly believing He is from God and acknowledging Him as Lord of your life! Despite the fact that Judas walked for years with Jesus, he never acknowledged Him as Lord. When Judas approached Jesus in the garden to betray Him, he addressed Him as "master", which means "great teacher". He did not call him Lord.

What do *you* say of the Lord? Is He just a man to you? Do you view Him only as a prophet or great teacher? Or do you confess Him as the Lord of your life? Can you truly say, "He is *my* God!"

As we close this chapter, make the Message Bible translation of this verse we have been studying your declaration:

*"Say this: 'God, you're my refuge.
I trust in you and I'm safe!'" (MSG)*

Chapter Four
Trusting In Him

"... in Him I will trust."

Trust is essential if you are to remain in the secret place. The English words *trust* and *true* both originated from the old Anglo-Saxon word, *trow*. Trust means to rely on the integrity of someone who is true, honest, and faithful. "Trust" in Old Testament Hebrew means "to take refuge in" and in the Greek New Testament it means "to confide and have faith in."

In Psalm 91:2, the psalmist declares *"In Him will I trust,"* referring to the Most High Almighty God of whom this passage speaks. The Amplified Bible translates this passage as: *"I will say of the Lord, He is my Refuge and my Fortress, my God; on Him I lean and rely, and in Him I [confidently] trust!"* The Darby Bible says, *"I will confide in Him."*

Misplaced Trust

In times of trouble, you will turn to someone or something to trust. Sometimes, you will find your confidence is misplaced because the friends, finances, and plans in which you trusted failed. The Bible warns against misplacing your trust in:

People. The Bible declares, *"Trust ye not in a friend, put ye not confidence in a guide"...(Micah 7:5).* This does not mean you cannot share your needs with a Christian friend or ask for their help or prayers, but don't rely on them. Trust in God. Psalms 146:3 cautions, *"Put not your trust in princes, nor in the son of man, in whom there is no help".* People can be a blessing in times of trouble, but if you put your trust in them to solve your problems you will often be disappointed. Psalms 118:8-9 confirms that, *"It is better to trust in the Lord* *than to put confidence in man."* Jeremiah 17:5 warns that trusting in man can cause your heart to depart from the Lord.

Money. Some people think they can buy their way out of trouble and that money is the solution to every problem. But the Apostle Paul cautioned, *"Charge them that are rich in this world, that they be not highminded, nor trust in uncertain riches, but in the living God, who giveth us richly all things to enjoy" (1 Timothy 6:17).*

Your own strength. Do not rely on your own strength in times of trouble. The Psalmist declared, *"... I will not trust in my bow, neither shall my sword save me" (Psalm 44:6).* He said *"Some trust in chariots, and some in horses: but we will remember the name of the Lord our God. They are brought down and fallen: but we are risen, and stand upright" (Psalm 20:7-8).* Bows, swords, chariots, and horses were common things that people relied on in Bible times and are symbolic of trusting in your own strength, plans, and abilities in times of trouble.

Oppression. The Bible also warns that you should *"Trust not in oppression..." (Psalm 62:10)*, meaning do not place your trust in any sort of wrong-doing. Do not think you can solve your problems by oppressing others, making them subservient to you, or extorting their property or services.

The Benefits Of Trusting God

The Psalmist spoke much about trusting because he learned to trust God at an early age. He said, *"For thou art my hope, O Lord God: thou art my trust from my youth" (Psalm 71:5).* He admonished the people to *"offer the sacrifices of righteousness, and put your trust in the Lord" (Psalm 4:5)* and declared that those who trust God are blessed (Psalm

2:12). He also said that God was the rock in which he would trust (2 Samuel 22:3).

Here are some powerful passages that emphasize the blessings that result from trusting God.

You have a refuge: *Trust in him at all times; ye people, pour out your heart before him: God is a refuge for us. Selah. (Psalms 62:8)*

You are able to declare God's works: *But it is good for me to draw near to God: I have put my trust in the Lord God, that I may declare all thy works. (Psalms 73:28)*

You have an answer for your enemies: *So shall I have wherewith to answer him that reproacheth me: for I trust in thy word. (Psalms 119:42)*

You are not alone in your difficulties: *And they that know thy name will put their trust in thee: for thou, Lord, hast not forsaken them that seek thee. (Psalms 9:10)*

The Lord redeemeth the soul of his servants: and none of them that trust in him shall be desolate. (Psalms 34:22)

But mine eyes are unto thee, O God the Lord: in thee is my trust; leave not my soul destitute. (Psalms 141:8)

You are delivered from the enemy: *...O Lord my God, in thee do I put my trust: save me from all them that persecute me, and deliver me... (Psalms 7:1)*

Shew thy marvellous lovingkindness, O thou that savest by thy right hand them which put their trust in thee from those that rise up against them. (Psalms 17:7)

And the Lord shall help them and deliver them: he shall deliver them from the wicked, and save them, because they trust in him. (Psalms 37:40)

The righteous shall be glad in the Lord, and shall trust in him; and all the upright in heart shall glory. (Psalms 64:10)

My goodness, and my fortress; my high tower, and my deliverer; my shield, and he in whom I trust; who subdueth my people under me. (Psalms 144:2)

Your are directed by God: *Trust in the Lord with all thine heart; and lean not unto thine own understanding. In all thy ways acknowledge him, and he shall direct thy paths. (Proverbs 3:5-6)*

Cause me to hear thy lovingkindness in the morning; for in thee do I trust: cause me to know the way wherein I should walk; for I lift up my soul unto thee. (Psalms 143:8)

Commit thy way unto the Lord; trust also in him; and he shall bring it to pass. (Psalms 37:5)

You have freedom from fear: *What time I am afraid, I will trust in thee. (Psalms 56:3)*

In God I will praise his word, in God I have put my trust; I will not fear what flesh can do unto me. (Psalms 56:4)

In God have I put my trust: I will not be afraid what man can do unto me. (Psalms 56:11)

Behold, God is my salvation; I will trust, and not be afraid: for the Lord Jehovah is my strength and my song; he also is become my salvation. (Isaiah 12:2)

You are free from shame: *O my God, I trust in thee: let me not be ashamed, let not mine enemies triumph over me. (Psalms 25:2)*

O keep my soul, and deliver me: let me not be ashamed; for I put my trust in thee. (Psalms 25:20)

In thee, O Lord, do I put my trust; let me never be ashamed: deliver me in thy righteousness. (Psalms 31:1)

You are filled with joy and praise: *But let all those that put their trust in thee rejoice: let them ever shout for joy, because thou defendest them: let them also that love thy name be joyful in thee. (Psalms 5:11)*

And he hath put a new song in my mouth, even praise unto our God: many shall see it, and fear, and shall trust in the Lord. (Psalms 40:3)

You have light in times of darkness: *Who is among you that feareth the Lord, that obeyeth the voice of his servant, that walketh in darkness, and hath no light? Let him trust in the name of the Lord, and stay upon his God. (Isaiah 50:10)*

Mercy is extended to you: *But I am like a green olive tree in the house of God: I trust in the mercy of God for ever and ever. (Psalms 52:8)*

There is no confusion: *In thee, O Lord, do I put my trust: let me never be put to confusion. (Psalms 71:1)*

God preserves you: *Preserve me, O God: for in thee do I put my trust. (Psalms 16:1)*

God protects you: *As for God, his way is perfect: the word of the Lord is tried: he is a buckler to all those that trust in him. (Psalms 18:30)*

The Lord is my rock, and my fortress, and my deliverer; my God, my strength, in whom I will trust; my buckler, and the horn of my salvation, and my high tower. (Psalms 18:2)

...trust thou in the Lord: he is their help and their shield. (Psalms 115:9)

Every word of God is pure: he is a shield unto them that put their trust in him. (Proverbs 30:5)

There is divine provision: *Trust in the Lord, and do good; so shalt thou dwell in the land, and verily thou shalt be fed. (Psalms 37:3)*

You are safe: *The fear of man bringeth a snare: but whoso putteth his trust in the Lord shall be safe. (Proverbs 29:25)*

You have a spiritual inheritance: *...he that putteth his trust in me shall possess the land, and shall inherit my holy mountain...(Isaiah 57:13)*

You learn stability: *They that trust in the Lord shall be as mount Zion, which cannot be removed, but abideth for ever. (Psalms 125:1)*

In the Lord put I my trust: How say ye to my soul, Flee as a bird to your mountain? (Psalms 11:1)

Goodness is stored up for you: *Oh how great is thy goodness, which thou hast laid up for them that fear thee;*

which thou hast wrought for them that trust in thee before the sons of men! (Psalms 31:19)

The Lord is your strength: *Trust ye in the Lord for ever: for in the Lord Jehovah is everlasting strength...(Isaiah 26:4)*

You have a spiritual stronghold: *The Lord is good, a stronghold in the day of trouble; and he knoweth them that trust in him. (Nahum 1:7)*

You will be happy: *...whoso trusteth in the Lord, happy is he. (Proverbs 16:20)*

With all of the tremendous blessings that result from trusting God, the question is, why wouldn't you want to trust Him?

Trusting In Every Circumstance

Throughout the Psalms, David repeatedly speaks of his trust in God. Note the various difficulties, problems, and circumstances in the following passage which are highlighted in bold-faced type:

> *Give ear to my prayer, O God; and hide not thyself from my supplication. Attend unto me, and hear me: I* **mourn in my complaint**, *and make a noise; Because of the* **voice of the enemy**, *because of the* **oppression of the wicked**: *for they cast* **iniquity** *upon me, and in* **wrath** *they* **hate** *me.* **My heart is sore pained** *within me: and the* **terrors of death** *are fallen upon me.* **Fearfulness** *and* **trembling** *are come upon me, and* **horror** *hath* **overwhelmed** *me. And I said, Oh that I had wings like a dove! for then would I fly away, and be at rest. Lo, then would I wander far off, and remain in the wilderness. Selah. I would hasten my escape from the* **windy storm and tempest**. *Destroy, O*

Lord, and divide their tongues: for I have seen **violence and strife** *in the city. Day and night they go about it upon the walls thereof:* **mischief also and sorrow** *are in the midst of it.* **Wickedness** *is in the midst thereof:* **deceit and guile** *depart not from her streets.* **For it was not an enemy that reproached me;** *then I could have borne it: neither was it he that* **hated me** *that* **did magnify himself against me;** *then I would have hid myself from him:* **But it was thou, a man mine equal, my guide, and mine acquaintance.** *We took sweet counsel together, and walked unto the house of God in company...The words of his mouth were smoother than butter, but* **war was in his heart:** **his words** *were softer than oil, yet were they* **drawn swords**... *But I will trust in thee.*
(Portions of Psalm 55:1-23)

What tremendous problems David was facing! Mourning, attacks of the enemy, oppression, iniquity, wrath, hatred, pain, terrors of death, fearfulness, trembling, horror, circumstances that felt like a windy storm and tempest, violence, strife, mischief, sorrow, wickedness, deceit, guile, and betrayal. Despite these tremendous challenges and difficulties, David declared: "I will trust in thee!"

Make that your declaration also, despite the negative circumstances, trouble, or suffering you may be experiencing. You previously studied about the importance of a proper confession, so declare right now: In Him I will trust...

> ...Despite my negative circumstances.
> ...Despite my broken heart.
> ...Despite my health.
> ...Despite my wayward friend or relative.
> ...Despite my lost finances...

...In Him will I trust!

Eternal Trust

You can always trust God because *"..he is the same yesterday, and to day, and for ever" (Hebrews 13:8)*. You can have confidence that there is *"no variableness, neither shadow of turning"* in Him (*James 1:17*). He won't be there for you one day and gone the next. He won't be unavailable or put you on hold when you call Him. As you will learn when you study verse 15 of Psalm 91, whenever you call, He will answer!

The Apostle Paul declared that the extreme difficulties he encountered resulted in him relying upon God rather than himself. He declared that God *"...delivered us from so great a death, and doth deliver: in whom we trust that he will yet deliver us" (2 Corinthians 1:10)*. Note that there is a past, present, and future aspect to this verse: He delivered in the past, He delivers in the present, and He will yet deliver!

-You trusted God in the past--and He delivered you. Just think of all He did for you in times gone by!

-You can trust Him in the present--because He does deliver.

-And you can trust God for the future and for all eternity, because *"...He will yet deliver you!"*

SECTION TWO
DIVINE PROTECTION

*"Surely He shall deliver you
from the snare of the fowler
and from the perilous pestilence.*

*He shall cover you with His feathers
and under His wings you shall take refuge;
His truth shall be your shield and buckler.*

*You shall not be afraid of
the terror by night,
Nor of the arrow that flies by day,
Nor of the pestilence
that walks in darkness,
Nor of the destruction
that lays waste at noonday.*

*A thousand may fall at your side,
and ten thousand by your right hand,
but it shall not come near you."*

(Psalm 91:3-7)

Chapter Five
Conquering Snares And Pestilence

"Surely He shall deliver you from the snare of the fowler and from the perilous pestilence."

Note the emphatic word of assurance--"surely"--that begins the promises of Psalm 91:3-7. The word means "for sure" or "truly". The word "surely" is used 284 times in the King James Version of the Bible to emphasize that a statement is true. "Without a doubt," the psalmist declares, "God will deliver you from the snare of the fowler and from the perilous pestilence."

Other versions translate this verse as follows:

-For it is He who delivers you from the snare of the trapper, And from the deadly pestilence. (NAS)

-He is the one who will rescue you from hunters' traps and from deadly plagues. (GWT)

-He Himself will deliver you from the hunter's net, from the destructive plague. (Holman Bible)

-God will save you from hidden traps and from deadly diseases. (NCV)

-For he will rescue you from every trap and protect you from the fatal plague. (NLT)

-That's right--he rescues you from hidden traps, shields you from deadly hazards. (MSG)

59

For He delivereth thee from the snare of a fowler,
From a calamitous pestilence. (Youngs)

As a believer who is dwelling in the secret place and abiding under the shadow of Almighty God, this promise of deliverance is yours! In order to claim it, however, you need to know:

> -What is deliverance?
> -Who is the fowler and what is his snare?
> -What is meant by perilous pestilence?

Deliverance

Man has a triune nature consisting of body, soul, and spirit. In this passage, God promises deliverance from snares and perilous pestilence which is inclusive of spiritual, physical, mental, and emotional attacks that may be launched against you by the enemy.

For too long the work of Satan and demons has been dismissed by many as a curious practice in heathen cultures rather than considered as that which commonly invades lives, homes, churches, and nations. But yet the Bible is clear that our enemies are Satan and his host of demonic powers.

There are people all around you who are tormented, troubled, and controlled by the powers of darkness known as demons. Part of the divine mandate of Christ's ministry was deliverance. He declared:

> *The Spirit of the Lord is upon me, because he hath anointed me to preach the gospel to the poor; he hath sent me to heal the brokenhearted, to **preach deliverance** to the captives, and recovering of sight to*

the blind, to set at liberty them that are bruised. (Luke 4:18)

Jesus ministered to those affected by demonic powers (Acts 10:38) and He commissioned His followers to do likewise as they spread the Gospel of the Kingdom (Matthew 10:1). Jesus declared:

> *And he said unto them, Go ye into all the world, and preach the gospel to every creature. He that believeth and is baptized shall be saved; but he that believeth not shall be damned. And these signs shall follow them that believe; In my name shall they cast out devils; they shall speak with new tongues; They shall take up serpents; and if they drink any deadly thing, it shall not hurt them; they shall lay hands on the sick, and they shall recover. (Mark 16:15-17)*

Jesus sent believers into the world, as He was sent forth (John 20:21), to do the works of God (John 14:12). He gave believers supernatural authority through His name to bring deliverance to those who are bound by demonic powers. "Deliverance" means to be set free from every controlling power of the enemy--sin, bondage, habits, strongholds, and all spiritual, mental, physical, and emotional problems.

How are believers to be delivered and minister this deliverance to others? Through the name of Jesus Christ! As this passage declares, *"...these signs shall follow them that believe; In my name shall they cast out devils."* God has secured your deliverance and--through the power of the name of Jesus Christ--you can extend His deliverance to those bound by the powers of the enemy. (You will learn more about the power of the God's name when you study Psalm 91:14.)

Repeatedly in the Psalms, David calls on God for help and declares the delivering power of Almighty God:

> *And the Lord shall help them and deliver them: he shall deliver them from the wicked, and save them, because they trust in him. (Psalm 37:40)*

> *And call upon me in the day of trouble: I will deliver thee, and thou shalt glorify me. (Psalm 50:15)*

Two more times in Psalm 91, the word "deliver" is used to emphasize God's desire to set you free from all the power of the enemy:

> *Because he hath set his love upon me, therefore will I **deliver** him: I will set him on high, because he hath known my name. He shall call upon me, and I will answer him: I will be with him in trouble; I will **deliver** him, and honour him. (Psalm 91:14-15)*

You will recall that the Apostle Paul spoke of a past, present, and future dimension of deliverance, declaring that God *"...delivered us from so great a death, and doth deliver: in whom we trust that he will yet deliver us..."* (2 Corinthians 1:10).

Paul also declares with assurance, *"And the Lord shall deliver me from every evil work, and will preserve me unto his heavenly kingdom: to whom be glory for ever and ever..."* (2 Timothy 4:18). The Apostle Peter adds that *"...the Lord knoweth how to deliver the godly out of temptations..."* (2 Peter 2:9),

The Snare Of The Fowler

Some believers think that if they walk with God, they will never face difficult times. This is not true because part of the daily prayer Jesus taught His followers to pray was *"deliver us from evil"* (Matthew 6:13). This means that each day you will be confronted with evil, snares, and pestilence from which you need deliverance.

In Psalm 91, God promises to deliver you from the snare of the fowler. The word "fowl" refers to birds and a "fowler" is a hunter, one who ensnares birds by a concealed trap. Other versions refer to the fowler's snare as a hunter's hidden traps. So the word "fowler", as used in this Psalm, refers to Satan, the enemy of all true believers, who desires to ensnare them in concealed traps. Paul refers to these as the "snares of the enemy" in 1 Timothy 3:7.

These snares are designed to hinder you from fulfilling your divine destiny. Satan is familiar with you--this is why the Bible speaks of "familiar spirits". Satan sets traps specifically designed for you. Just like hunting in the animal kingdom, what works to ensnare one type of animal will not work on another. A bear trap won't ensnare a bird. The bird just eats the bait and flies off. A snare designed for a bird won't capture a bear because it is too small and has the wrong bait. A different trap is used for different species.

This is true spiritually also. For one person, the snare of the enemy comes in the form of a person. For someone else, it is the love of money which becomes such a motivating force that they begin to make decisions based solely on financial gain. Others are tempted to sacrifice destiny for security.

A snare is always concealed, which means you don't know that it is there. This is why you must learn how to walk continuously in God's shadow and dwell in His presence so He can guide you around the snares. You can't just spend a few minutes in prayer in the morning and then go your own way and do your own thing the remainder of the day. You must continually walk with God so that He can help you avoid the snares of the enemy. In fact, sometimes you may never even know the snares were there. Many times, you will travel down the pathway to your destiny, walking in the shadow of the Almighty, oblivious of the snares from which He has delivered you.

Remember, a snare is concealed. You don't know you are stepping into it. You don't know how and when a snare is coming. Just ask a soldier who has inadvertently stepped on a hidden land mine.

Here are some specific spiritual snares identified in the Bible:

Snares set by others: *"The wicked have laid a snare for me: yet I erred not from thy precepts" (Psalm 119:110); "They...have hid a snare for me..." (Psalm 142:3).*

Idolatry: This not only means actual idols, but anything that comes between you and God: *"And they served their idols: which were a snare unto them" (Psalm 106:36).*

Your own mouth: *"A fool's mouth is his destruction, and his lips are the snare of his soul" (Proverbs 18:7).*

Your companions: The Bible warns, *"Make no friendship with an angry man; and with a furious man thou shalt not go: Lest thou learn his ways, and get a snare to thy soul" (Proverbs 22:24-25).* You can substitute any negative word for "angry" and this verse will remain true. Don't be friends with a dishonest man, lest you learn his ways. Don't be friends with a violent man, an abusive person, an addict, etc.-- lest you learn their ways and the relationship becomes a snare to you.

The fear of man: The Bible warns that *"The fear of man bringeth a snare: but whoso putteth his trust in the Lord shall be safe" (Proverbs 29:25).* Undue concern over what others think or say about you or what they might do to you will entrap you in a snare.

A bad reputation: A bad reputation, especially among unbelievers, is a snare: *"Moreover he must have a good report of them which are without; lest he fall into reproach and the snare of the devil" (1 Timothy 3:7).*

Riches: It is not money itself, but rather the love of money that results in a snare: *"But they that will be rich fall into temptation and a snare, and into many foolish and hurtful lusts, which drown men in destruction and perdition. For the love of money is the root of all evil: which while some coveted after, they have erred from the faith, and pierced themselves through with many sorrows" (1 Timothy 6:9-10).*

Snares set by the enemy: This one pretty much covers every other kind of snare not mentioned in the previous categories. *"And that they may recover themselves out of the snare of the devil, who are taken captive by him at his will" (2 Timothy 2:26).*

The Bible warns that Satan is roaming around seeking those he can devour:

> *Be sober, be vigilant; because your adversary the devil, as a roaring lion, walketh about, seeking whom he may devour: Whom resist stedfast in the faith,*

knowing that the same afflictions are accomplished in your brethren that are in the world. (1 Peter 5:8-9)

Why does Satan have to seek those whom he can devour? Because some of us are walking in God's shadow and we won't be snared. Not everyone gets caught. Satan seeks out and devours those who are not living under the shadow of the Almighty. They are walking their own way and doing their own thing. By distancing themselves from God, they become easy prey.

When God makes you aware of a snare, then resist the enemy steadfastly in a faith that is firmly rooted in the Word of God because: *"The law of the wise is a fountain of life, To turn one away from the snares of death"* (Proverbs 13:14, NKJV).

The Bible also declares, *"Deliver thyself as a roe from the hand of the hunter, and as a bird from the hand of the fowler"* (Proverbs 6:5). God promises deliverance, but believers have a part in the process to *"...recover themselves out of the snare of the devil, who are taken captive by him at his will"* (2 Timothy 2:26).

Make a declaration right now to resist the enemy in faith and recover yourself from any snares into which you may have strayed by not walking in God's shadow. In the future, when snares are revealed to you by the Holy Spirit, avoid them and remain in your place of safety in the shadow of Almighty God.

Pray this prayer each day:

> *...My eyes are upon You, O God the Lord; In You I take refuge; Do not leave my soul destitute. Keep me from the snares they have laid for me, And from the*

traps of the workers of iniquity. Let the wicked fall into their own nets, While I escape safely. (Psalm 141:8-10, NKJ)

Then you can declare in victory, *"Blessed be the Lord, who hath not given us as a prey to their teeth. Our soul is escaped as a bird out of the snare of the fowlers: the snare is broken, and we are escaped" (Psalm 124:6-7).*

Perilous Pestilence

The word "perilous" means dangerous. The word "pestilence" is defined as "any deadly infection or malady." Not only will God deliver you from the concealed snares of the enemy, He will deliver you from physical, mental, and emotional attacks. Other versions translate the "perilous pestilence" as deadly, destructive, fatal plagues, calamitous pestilence, and deadly hazards.

The Almighty God in whose shadow you dwell has promised:

...If thou wilt diligently hearken to the voice of the Lord thy God, and wilt do that which is right in His sight, and wilt give ear to His commandments, and keep all His statues, I will put none of these diseases upon thee, which I have brought upon the Egyptians; for I am the Lord that healeth thee. (Exodus 15:26)

Isaiah 53 is a prophetic chapter concerning Jesus Christ. Verses four and five definitely link healing to the atonement of Jesus through His death on the cross:

Surely, He hath borne our griefs, and carried our sorrows; yet we did esteem Him stricken, smitten of God, and afflicted. But He was wounded for our transgressions, He was bruised for our iniquities; the chastisement of our peace was upon Him; and with His stripes we are healed. (Isaiah 53:4-5)

The only use of the word "surely" in this chapter--which is a word of emphasis--precedes this provision for your salvation and healing. It is the same word used in Psalm 91:3 when the psalmist declares that surely God will deliver you from pestilence.

Sin and sickness are Satan's twin evils. Salvation and healing are God's twin provisions for deliverance. Before Jesus Christ died people were saved and healed by looking forward to the cross in faith. Afterwards, salvation and healing come by looking back to the cross in faith and accepting Christ's sacrifice for sin, sickness, sorrow, and shame.

Disease and death entered the world by sin and resulted as penalties for iniquity, so their remedies must be found in the atonement of Christ. Jesus bore your sicknesses and carried your diseases at the same time and in the same manner that He bore your sins:

> *That it might be fulfilled which was spoken by Esaias the prophet, saying, Himself took our infirmities and bare our sicknesses. (Matthew 8:17)*

God laid both sin and sickness on Jesus in the same atonement. Peter speaks of salvation and healing as an accomplished fact:

> *Who His own self bare our sins in His own body on the tree, that we, being dead to sins, should live unto righteousness: by whose stripes ye were healed.*
> *(1 Peter 2:24)*

The same God who forgives your sin also heals your diseases:

> *Bless the Lord, O my soul, and forget not all His benefits: Who forgiveth all thine iniquities, who healeth all thy diseases. (Psalms 103:2-3)*

The name "Jehovah-tsidkenu" reveals God's redemptive provision for your soul. The name "Jehovah-rapha" reveals His redemptive provision for your body.

The word "saved" in Romans 10:9 is the same word used by the disciple Mark when he said "as many as touched him were made whole" (Mark 6:56). The Greek word "*sozo*" used in these passages means salvation from sin and its penalty. Sickness is part of the penalty, so salvation is the atonement for it.

When Jesus died on the cross did He take away your sins? Do you, as a believer, still battle against sin? The answer to both questions is "yes!" The same is true of sickness. Jesus died for your sickness, but as long as you are in an imperfect world where Satan is active, you will also war against sickness.

There is a past, present, and future tense of salvation:

-Past: You are saved from the penalty of sins
committed in the past.
-Present: You are saved from the power of sin in
the present.
-Future: You will be saved from the presence of sin
in the future (eternity).

The same is true of sickness. You are saved from the penalty of disease for your sin. You can overcome the power of disease in the present and you will be saved from the actual presence of disease when you pass into eternity.

It is evident that the promise to deliver from the "noisome pestilence" applies to physical attacks of the enemy, but it can also apply to bitterness, anger, and hatred. These are deadly emotional maladies that affect you mentally, spiritually, and physically.

If you dwell in the secret place continually and abide under the shadow of Almighty God, you will not harbor these negative emotions because bitterness, anger, and hatred all stem from unforgiveness. Jesus emphasized the importance of forgiveness and forgiving others in the prayer that He taught His disciples:

> *Give us day by day our daily bread. And forgive us our sins; for we also forgive every one that is indebted to us. And lead us not into temptation; but deliver us from evil. (Luke 11:3-4)*

You only harm yourself when you refuse to forgive. Unforgiveness becomes a "noisome pestilence" where you continually rehearse the wrongs done to you. The Lord's emphasis on forgiving others is not only because it is morally right to forgive, but also because it is vital for spiritual, physical, and mental health. People who refuse to forgive are harboring perilous pestilence in their lives--deadly spiritual and emotional infections from which God wants to deliver them.

The fact that forgiveness needs to be received and given each day is evident because it is a prayer pattern to be followed daily--"Give us this day our daily bread." Not only is divine provision needed daily, so is the divine ability to receive and extend forgiveness.

The atonement of Jesus Christ guarantees a believer's final perfection, but for the time physical, mental, emotional, and spiritual imperfections continue because we live in a sinful world. The believer is not immune to attacks of sin and sickness because the ultimate benefits of Christ's atonement are yet to be revealed. You are, however, *"...kept by the power of God through faith unto salvation ready to be revealed in the last time" (1 Peter 1:5).* The benefits of salvation yet to be revealed in eternity are those of physical, mental, emotional, and spiritual perfection.

Although you are not immune to these attacks, you have spiritual weapons and the resident power of God within you to face them without fear. You also have a place of protection under the wings of God which you will learn about in the next chapter.

Chapter Six
Taking Refuge Under His Wings

"He shall cover you with His feathers and under His wings you shall take refuge..."

In Psalm 91, the psalmist declared his trust in God and you learned what it means to trust the Lord as you studied verse two. Now, in the first portion of verse four, the psalmist declares his trust again, this time in the covering provided by the feathers and wings of God:

> -*[Then] He will cover you with His pinions, and under His wings shall you trust and find refuge...* (AMP)

> -*His huge outstretched arms protect you--under them you're perfectly safe; his arms fend off all harm.* (MSG)

> -*With his shoulders he shall make shadow to thee; and thou shalt have hope under his feathers. His truth shall (en)compass thee with a shield; (With his feathers he shall make a shadow for thee; and thou shalt have hope under his wings. His faithfulness shall surround thee like a shield.)* (Wycliff)

The question this verse raises is, what is meant by the feathers and wings of God?

When we think of wings, we visualize the wings of a bird or wings we have seen in artistic renditions of angels. Whether or not God actually appears to have wings is not the point. The important thing is that the analogy used here of being covered by His feathers and wings is one of the most tender expressions of God's care in all of scripture. God responds towards His children as a bird does to her brood, taking us under His spiritual wings and feathers to shelter us from danger.

While sitting on a hillside overlooking Jerusalem Jesus lamented:

> *O Jerusalem, Jerusalem, which killest the prophets, and stonest them that are sent unto thee; how often would I have gathered thy children together, as a hen doth gather her brood under her wings, and ye would not! (Luke 13:34)*

Note that the refuge of God's wings is available and it is the Lord's desire that you find shelter there, but you must make the choice to do so. What sad words, that Jesus wanted to shelter His people but *"they would not."*

David made a decision to dwell continually under God's wings. He declared, *"I will abide in thy tabernacle for ever: I will trust in the covert of thy wings" (Psalm 61:4)*. He also said:

> *Because You have been my help, Therefore in the shadow of Your wings I will rejoice. My soul follows close behind You; Your right hand upholds me. (Psalm 63:7-8, NKJV)*

Because God had been his help in times past, David trusted and rejoiced under the shadow of His wings. The psalmist declared, *"My soul follows close behind you."* You studied previously about abiding in God's shadow. This is the only way to remain close enough to find shelter beneath His wings.

By natural instinct, a bird protects its young by gathering them under her wings. She calls them there when she senses danger and it is there that they are kept safe from harm. Using this great analogy, God compares it to His care for His people who are in need of comfort and protection from the enemy.

It is under the wings of God's protection that you come to know His loving-kindness:

> *How excellent is thy lovingkindness, O God! therefore the children of men put their trust under the shadow of thy wings. (Psalm 36:7)*

The psalmist lists additional blessings that are found under God's wings when he prays:

> *Be merciful unto me, O God, be merciful unto me: for my soul trusteth in thee: yea, in the shadow of thy wings will I make my refuge, until these calamities be overpast. I will cry unto God most high; unto God that performeth all things for me. He shall send from heaven, and save from the reproach of him that would swallow me up. Selah. God shall send forth his mercy and his truth. (Psalm 57:1-3)*

From this passage we learn that under God's wings:
-Mercy is extended to you.
-You will find refuge.
-You are protected from calamities.
-You can cry to God and He will answer in all
 things pertaining to you.
-He will save you from reproach.
-He will protect you from being swallowed up by
 the enemy.

-His mercy and truth will be sent forth in your
behalf.

The psalmist prayed, *"Keep me as the apple of the eye, hide
me under the shadow of thy wings from the wicked that
oppress me, from my deadly enemies, who compass me
about" (Psalm 17:8-9).* From this request we learn that
under God's wings there is shelter from the wicked, from
oppression, and from deadly enemies that surround you.

There is healing under the wings of God--not only for
physical conditions, but spiritual healing for sin, negative
emotions, and deep hurts:

> *But unto you that fear my name shall the Sun of
> righteousness arise with healing in his wings; and ye
> shall go forth, and grow up as calves of the stall.
> (Malachi 4:2)*

Those who experience shelter under God's wings--no matter
how great their difficulties--will be able to go forth again
rejoicing like a calf let out of a stall.

God's wings also bear you up in times of trouble. God
reminded Israel, *"Ye have seen what I did unto the Egyptians,
and how I bare you on eagles' wings, and brought you unto
myself" (Exodus 19:4).* Using the metaphor of an eagle, God
is represented as carrying the Israelites on His wings during
their wilderness journey:

> *As an eagle stirreth up her nest, fluttereth over her
> young, spreadeth abroad her wings, taketh them,
> beareth them on her wings: So the Lord alone did
> lead him, and there was no strange god with him. He
> made him ride on the high places of the earth, that he
> might eat the increase of the fields; and he made him*

to suck honey out of the rock, and oil out of the flinty
rock. (Deuteronomy 32:11-12)

If you are going through a wilderness experience right now,
you can find shelter under the wings of God. Let Him bear
you up through the barren days ahead. He will lead you,
protect you, and provide for you as He did for Israel:

> *Hast thou not known? hast thou not heard, that the*
> *everlasting God, the Lord, the Creator of the ends of*
> *the earth, fainteth not, neither is weary? there is no*
> *searching of his understanding. He giveth power to*
> *the faint; and to them that have no might he*
> *increaseth strength. Even the youths shall faint and be*
> *weary, and the young men shall utterly fall: But they*
> *that wait upon the Lord shall renew their strength;*
> *they shall mount up with wings as eagles; they shall*
> *run, and not be weary; and they shall walk, and not*
> *faint. (Isaiah 40:28-31)*

If you are feeling faint today--whether it be mentally,
spiritually, emotionally or physically--let God bear you up on
His wings. He will renew your strength so that you can rise
up with wings as eagles and run the race set before you
without growing weary.

The Ark of the Tabernacle, which represented the presence of
God, had carvings of angelic cherubim with wings. When an
Israelite sinned, forgiveness was to be sought beneath these
wings at the altar of the Lord. Under His wings there is
forgiveness and safety. The psalmist prayed:

Please God, show me mercy!
Open your grace-fountain for me,
For you are my soul's true Shelter.
I will hide beneath the shadow of your embrace,
Under the wings of your cherubim
Until this terrible trouble is past. (Psalm 57:1, TPT)

God rules enthroned between the wings of the cherubim. (Psalm 99:1, TPT). If you are being attacked by the enemy, seek shelter under God's wings. If you need healing, you will find it there. If you need mercy, forgiveness, and love--come under God's wings. If you need protection from reproach and calamities, seek shelter there. Be covered by the wings and feathers of God.

Chapter Seven
Appropriating God's Truth

"His truth shall be your shield and buckler."

As you learned in the last chapter, wings speak of God's compassion, warmth, and comfort. The shield and buckler mentioned in Psalm 91:4 represent His strength.

As you are strengthened and comforted under God's wings, His truth empowers you to emerge as a fully-equipped Christian soldier with a protective spiritual shield and buckler firmly in place: *"His truth shall be your shield and buckler."*

If you are to appropriate the blessings of His truth, you must determine:

-What is His truth?
-What are the benefits of His truth?
-What is your shield?
-What is your buckler?

His Truth

It is not a scientific, geological, or mathematic theory spoken of in Psalm 91:4. It is *His* truth! The verse declares that *His* truth shall be your shield and buckler. Pilate posed the question, *"What is truth?" (John 18:38).* But when confronted with the truth standing right in front of him manifested in Jesus Christ, Pilate rejected it. Are you ready to receive the revelation of His truth?

To learn the meaning of His truth, we look to God's Word where we discover that:

God is truth: *He is...a God of truth and without iniquity, just and right is he. (Deuteronomy 32:4)*

Jesus Christ is truth: *Jesus saith unto him, I am the way, the truth, and the life: no man cometh unto the Father, but by me. (John 14:6)*

The Holy Spirit is the Spirit of truth: *Even the Spirit of truth; whom the world cannot receive, because it seeth him not, neither knoweth him: but ye know him; for he dwelleth with you, and shall be in you. (John 14:17)*

God's Word is truth: *Thy word is true from the beginning... (Psalm 119:160)*

God's laws are truth: *Thy righteousness is an everlasting righteousness, and thy law is the truth. (Psalms 119:142)*

God's commandments are truth: *Thou art near, O Lord; and all thy commandments are truth. (Psalms 119:151)*

The Gospel is truth: *For the hope which is laid up for you in heaven, whereof ye heard before in the word of the truth of the gospel. (Colossians 1:5)*

The works of the Lord are done in truth: *For the word of the Lord is right; and all his works are done in truth. (Psalms 33:4)*

God's counsel is truth: *O Lord, thou art my God; I will exalt thee, I will praise thy name; for thou hast done wonderful things; thy counsels of old are faithfulness and truth. (Isaiah 25:1)*

The judgments of the Lord are truth: *The fear of the Lord is clean, enduring for ever: the judgments of the Lord are true and righteous altogether. (Psalms 19:9)*

The church is the pillar and ground of truth: *But if I tarry long, that thou mayest know how thou oughtest to behave thyself in the house of God, which is the church of the living God, the pillar and ground of the truth. (1 Timothy 3:15)*

The anointing within you is truth: *But the anointing which ye have received of him abideth in you, and ye need not that any man teach you: but as the same anointing teacheth you of all things, and is truth, and is no lie, and even as it hath taught you, ye shall abide in him. (1 John 2:27)*

The Benefits Of His Truth

David recognized the tremendous benefits of God's truth. He prayed, *"Lead me in thy truth, and teach me: for thou art the God of my salvation; on thee do I wait all the day" (Psalm 25:5).* Here are some of the benefits of His truth.

His truth stands the test of time: *For the Lord is good; his mercy is everlasting; and his truth endureth to all generations. (Psalm 100:5)*

His truth is dependable: *For ever, O Lord, thy word is settled in heaven. (Psalm 119:89)*

His truth will set you free: *And ye shall know the truth, and the truth shall make you free. (John 8:32)*

His truth preserves you: *Withhold not thou thy tender mercies from me, O Lord: let thy lovingkindness and thy truth continually preserve me. (Psalms 40:11)*

His truth leads you: *O send out thy light and thy truth: let them lead me; let them bring me unto thy holy hill, and to thy tabernacles. (Psalms 43:3)*

His truth is plenteous: *But thou, O Lord, art a God full of compassion, and gracious, longsuffering, and plenteous in mercy and truth. (Psalms 86:15)*

His truth judges you fairly: *...for he cometh to judge the earth: he shall judge the world with righteousness, and the people with his truth. (Psalms 96:13)*

He is near those who call upon Him in truth: *The Lord is nigh unto all them that call upon him, to all that call upon him in truth. (Psalms 145:18)*

His truth purges your iniquity: *By mercy and truth iniquity is purged: and by the fear of the Lord men depart from evil. (Proverbs 16:6)*

His truth enables you to worship God: *But the hour cometh, and now is, when the true worshippers shall worship the Father in spirit and in truth: for the Father seeketh such to worship him. God is a Spirit: and they that worship him must worship him in spirit and in truth. (John 4:23-24)*

The Spirit of truth guides you into all truth: *Howbeit when he, the Spirit of truth, is come, he will guide you into all truth: for he shall not speak of himself; but whatsoever he shall hear, that shall he speak: and he will shew you things to come. (John 16:13)*

You are sanctified through the truth: *Sanctify them through thy truth: thy word is truth. (John 17:17)*

You are chosen for salvation because of your belief in the truth: *But we are bound to give thanks alway to God for you, brethren beloved of the Lord, because God hath from the beginning chosen you to salvation through sanctification of the Spirit and belief of the truth. (2 Thessalonians 2:13)*

The truth establishes you: *Wherefore I will not be negligent to put you always in remembrance of these things, though ye know them, and be established in the present truth. (2 Peter 1:12)*

His truth is your shield and buckler: *His truth shall be your shield and buckler (Psalm 91:4)*--two powerful benefits we will examine in detail later in this chapter.

With all of these benefits of God's truth, it is easy to understand why the scriptures advise, *"Let not mercy and truth forsake thee: bind them about thy neck; write them upon the table of thine heart" (Proverbs 3:3).*

The Bible declares that it is God's will that all men be saved and come to the knowledge of the truth (1 Timothy 2:4). As believers we are admonished to *"Study to shew thyself approved unto God, a workman that needeth not to be ashamed, rightly dividing the word of truth" (2 Timothy 2:15).*

The Bible warns of those who have departed from the truth, rejected it, embraced fables and traditions of man, and are ever learning but never able to come to the knowledge of the truth. Satan, is deceptive. He was *"...a murderer from the beginning, and abode not in the truth, because there is no truth in him. When he speaketh a lie, he speaketh of his own: for he is a liar, and the father of it" (John 8:44).*

Here are some examples of the deceptions that the father of lies, Satan, perpetrates:

-Satan says, "God doesn't love you." God says you cannot be separated from His love:

> *Who shall separate us from the love of Christ? shall tribulation, or distress, or persecution, or famine, or nakedness, or peril, or sword? As it is written, For thy sake we are killed all the day long; we are accounted as sheep for the slaughter. Nay, in all these things we are more than conquerors through him that loved us. For I am persuaded, that neither death, nor life, nor angels, nor principalities, nor powers, nor things present, nor things to come, Nor height, nor depth, nor any other creature, shall be able to separate us from the love of God, which is in Christ Jesus our Lord. (Romans 8:35-39)*

-Satan says, "You will never amount to anything." God says He will complete His good work in you:

> *Being confident of this very thing, that he which hath begun a good work in you will perform it until the day of Jesus Christ. (Philippians 1:6)*

-Satan says, "You are insignificant." God says you are His workmanship:

> *For we are his workmanship, created in Christ Jesus unto good works, which God hath before ordained that we should walk in them. (Ephesians 2:10)*

-Satan says "God won't listen to you." God says you have access to His presence:

Let us therefore come boldly unto the throne of grace, that we may obtain mercy, and find grace to help in time of need. (Hebrews 4:16)

-Satan says, "You are not acceptable to God." God says you are His child:

But as many as received him, to them gave he power to become the sons of God, even to them that believe on his name. (John 1:12)

-Satan says, "You can't do anything right." God says you can do all things:

I can do all things through Christ which strengtheneth me. (Philippians 4:13)

-Satan says, "No one values you." God says you are bought with a price:

What? know ye not that your body is the temple of the Holy Ghost which is in you, which ye have of God, and ye are not your own? For ye are bought with a price: therefore glorify God in your body, and in your spirit, which are God's. (1 Corinthians 6:19-20)

Whenever Satan attacks your mind with lies, meditate on the truths of the Word of God rather than the lies he is telling you:

Finally, brethren, whatsoever things are true, whatsoever things are honest, whatsoever things are just, whatsoever things are pure, whatsoever things are lovely, whatsoever things are of good report; if there be any virtue, and if there be any praise, think on these things. (Philippians 4:8)

Your Shield

We have examined the meaning of His truth. Now we need to understand the concept of a shield and buckler. The psalmist declares to those living in the secret place, *"His truth will be your shield and buckler."* One version renders this passage *"His truth will encompass thee with armor" (Sept).* "Encompass" means to surround you totally. Another version states that *"His faithful promises are your armor" (Tay).*

In the natural world in Bible times, a shield was used to provide protection to the warrior's entire body. Even today, in riotous conditions you will see law enforcement personnel carrying full body shields which they hold in front of them to deflect attacks.

The Roman shields were made of six layers of animal hide that were woven together. The shield had to be oiled daily or else it would begin to crack and fall apart. In the spirit world, the truth--also called the shield of faith--provides complete protection spiritually. Truth is part of your spiritual armor, as Psalm 91:4 declares, *"His truth shall be your shield and buckler."* As the Roman soldiers cared for their shields, you must also care for your spiritual shield daily by immersing yourself in the Word of God.

After listing the various components of the Christian's spiritual armor, the Apostle Paul declares, *"Above all, taking the shield of faith, wherewith ye shall be able to quench all the fiery darts of the wicked" (Ephesians 6:16).* Nothing the enemy hurls at you will be effective when you have your shield of faith in place. But note that you must take it. "Taking" is an active word implying continuous action. The shield of faith is the truth of God's Word and the continual application of the Word to the circumstances of life. It is a shield that protects you from the evil forces in the world:

For whatsoever is born of God overcometh the world; and this is the victory that overcometh the world, even our faith. (1 John 5:4)

The Bible speaks of saving faith, the gift of faith, and the spiritual fruit of faith. But the word "faith" when used in relation to the shield of faith indicates the truth of the Word, a firm trust and confidence in God which protects your whole spiritual being. It protects you from flaming missiles of doubt and unbelief launched by the enemy. It is a calm and confident trust in God which deflects all the fiery arrows of the enemy from reaching their targets.

God first revealed this spiritual shield to Abram in Genesis 15:1 when He declared, *"Fear not, Abram: I am thy shield..."* The nation of Israel acknowledged God as the shield of their help (Deuteronomy 33:29). David repeatedly referred to God as his shield (Psalm 3:3; 28:7; 33:20; 35:2; 84:9,11).

The shield is related to salvation. David declared, *"Thou hast also given me the shield of thy salvation"... (Psalms 18:35).* The favor of God that surrounds the righteous is part of this spiritual shield, as the Bible declares: *"For thou, Lord, wilt bless the righteous; with favour wilt thou compass him as with a shield" (Psalms 5:12).* Those who trust in the Lord are helped and shielded by Him:

Ye that fear the Lord, trust in the Lord: he is their help and their shield. (Psalms 115:11)

The Word of God--His truth--is your shield. Proverbs 30:5 declares *"Every word of God is pure: he is a shield unto them that put their trust in him."* In Psalm 119:114, David relates the shield and the hiding place when he declares, *"Thou art my hiding place and my shield: I hope in thy word."*

The psalmist also relates the shield to deliverance. He declares that God is *"My goodness, and my fortress; my high tower, and my deliverer; my shield, and he in whom I trust..." (Psalm 144:2).*

So in summary, the shield of truth is your faith which you must continually renew through the Word of God. Your shield saves, protects, delivers, and surrounds you with God's favor.

Your Buckler

The Apostle Paul details the Christian soldier's spiritual armor in Ephesians 6:

> *Finally, my brethren, be strong in the Lord, and in the power of his might. Put on the whole armour of God, that ye may be able to stand against the wiles of the devil. For we wrestle not against flesh and blood, but against principalities, against powers, against the rulers of the darkness of this world, against spiritual wickedness in high places. Wherefore take unto you the whole armour of God, that ye may be able to withstand in the evil day, and having done all, to stand. Stand therefore, having your loins girt about with truth, and having on the breastplate of righteousness; And your feet shod with the preparation of the gospel of peace; Above all, taking the shield of faith, wherewith ye shall be able to quench all the fiery darts of the wicked. And take the helmet of salvation, and the sword of the Spirit, which is the word of God: Praying always with all prayer and supplication in the Spirit, and watching thereunto with all perseverance and supplication for all saints. (Ephesians 6:11-18)*

The first piece of armor to be put on is the girdle or belt of truth which is called the buckler. The buckler held all the other pieces of a soldier's armor in place. The truth of God's Word is your spiritual buckler to which all other pieces of your spiritual armor are attached. Your loins (representing your spiritual vital organs) must be girt (covered) with truth: *"Stand therefore, having your loins girt about with truth..." (Ephesians 6:14).* In Bible times, the buckler protected a soldier's reproductive organs. The same is true of your spiritual armor. If you are not protected by the belt of truth, you will be sterile spiritually.

All other components of your spiritual armor are vitally related to the truth. You cannot have the breastplate of righteousness in place without the buckler of truth. Your salvation (helmet) is based on the truth. Your sword is the truth of God's Word. Your faith (shield) is based upon that truth. Your spiritual shoes of the Gospel of peace also rely upon His truth.

You are not successful in spiritual battles because of your church fellowship, your small group membership, or your work for God. You are victorious because of the spiritual weapons and the power God has given you to overcome all the power of the enemy. The breastplate of righteousness, feet shod with the preparation of the Gospel of peace, the helmet of salvation, the shield of faith, the sword of the Spirit, and prayer--all function together properly because of God's truth.

Satan's first successful attack on mankind involved challenging God's truth:

> *And the woman said unto the serpent...God hath said, Ye shall not eat of it, neither shall ye touch it, lest ye*

die. And the serpent said unto the woman, Ye shall not surely die. (Genesis 3:2-4)

Satan also challenged the truth of God's Word when he tempted Jesus (Matthew 4:1-11). Satan's tactics have not changed after all these years. He still challenges the truth when he tempts you to sin. Only the buckler of truth can protect you! This is why you must study the Word of God so you are acquainted with the truth and you can wage effective spiritual warfare.

God is a tried and true buckler to those who trust Him. Because God has been tried and proven true, the buckler of His Word is also tried and true:

> *As for God, his way is perfect: the word of the Lord is tried: he is a buckler to all those that trust in him. (Psalms 18:30)*

The buckler of truth creates a strong fortress of spiritual deliverance and salvation:

> *The Lord is my rock, and my fortress, and my deliverer; my God, my strength, in whom I will trust; my buckler, and the horn of my salvation, and my high tower. (Psalms 18:2)*

The buckler protects those who live righteously:

> *He layeth up sound wisdom for the righteous: he is a buckler to them that walk uprightly. (Proverbs 2:7)*

The fact that God has equipped you with a shield and buckler indicates that you will face difficult times, despite the fact you are living in the secret place.

You need not fear these attacks, however, for one of the great promises of Psalm 91 is *"You shall not be afraid"*--and that is the subject of the next chapter.

Chapter Eight
Breaking The Spirit Of Fear

"You shall not be afraid of the terror by night,
Nor of the arrow that flies by day,
Nor of the pestilence that walks in darkness,
Nor of the destruction
that lays waste at noonday."

When you are dwelling in the secret place, *"You shall not be afraid of the terror of the night, nor of the arrow (the evil plots and slanders of the wicked) that flies by day. Nor of the pestilence that stalks in darkness, nor of the destruction and sudden death that surprise and lay waste at noonday."* (Psalm 91:5-6, AMP).

Three important concepts to note as you begin your study of this passage:

> -First, these promises are given to those who are dwelling in the secret place and abiding in the shadow of the Almighty (Psalm 91:1).

> -Second, this verse does not claim that you will not encounter terror, arrows, pestilence, and destruction, but it says you need not fear these things.

> -Third, the promise provides 24/7 protection including night, day, darkness, and noonday. The Jews divided the 24 hours of day and night into four parts: Evening, midnight, morning, and midday. You need not fear at any time because the One who cares for you never sleeps or slumbers (Psalm 121:4).

God's Word Translation speaks of *"plagues that roam in the dark, epidemics that strike at noon"* and the Good News Bible speaks of *"dangers at night and sudden attacks during the day...and evils that kill in daylight"*. The New Century Version says you will not fear dangers at night, arrows during the day, diseases, or sickness. The Message Bible declares: *"Fear nothing--not wild wolves in the night, not flying arrows in the day, Not disease that prowls through the darkness, not disaster that erupts at high noon"*.

The Wycliff Bible confirms: *"...thou shalt not dread of the night's dread. Of an arrow flying in the day, (Thou shalt not fear the terror in the night; nor an arrow flying in the day.) Of a goblin going in darknesses; of assailing, and of a midday fiend. (Nor the pestilence going in darkness; nor the assailing of the plague at midday.)"*

This chapter explores the subject of fear, presents biblical steps to alleviate fear, and discusses the spiritual meaning of terror, arrows, pestilence, and destruction.

Fear Is The Root

Fear is a powerful, controlling, paralyzing emotion. The dictionary defines fear as being fearful or scared of something. Fear fosters many irrational phobias and its most severe manifestations causes a person to withdraw from society and become agoraphobic--confined as a prisoner in their own home where they think they are safe.

Fear was first manifested after Adam and Eve sinned in the Garden of Eden. When God came seeking them in the cool of the day, Adam replied: *"...I heard thy voice in the garden, and I was afraid..." (Genesis 3:10)*. The first negative emotion resulting from sin was fear which was followed immediately by shame, isolation, blaming others, etc. As the first negative emotion experienced by man after the initial sin, fear is the root of all other negative emotions.

Medical science has proven that fear results in stress, high blood pressure, strokes, and heart attacks. The Bible speaks of men's hearts failing because of fear (Luke 21:26) and of people living in bondage all of their lives because of the fear of death (Hebrews 2:15).

Fear is a tormenting emotion (1 John 4:18). Its torment can include fearing suffering, loss of health, loss of a loved one, loss of wealth, abandonment, the future, death, and a host of other concerns.

God designed the universe to run on a 24-hour period of time. This is why the prayer Jesus taught His disciples was to be a daily prayer for needs to be provided--"Give us this day our daily bread." Fear results when you violate this principle and worry about the future:

> *Therefore I say unto you, Take no thought for your life, what ye shall eat, or what ye shall drink; nor yet for your body, what ye shall put on. Is not the life more than meat, and the body than raiment? Behold the fowls of the air: for they sow not, neither do they reap, nor gather into barns; yet your heavenly Father feedeth them. Are ye not much better than they? Which of you by taking thought can add one cubit unto his stature? And why take ye thought for raiment? Consider the lilies of the field, how they grow; they toil not, neither do they spin: And yet I say unto you, That even Solomon in all his glory was not arrayed like one of these. Wherefore, if God so clothe the grass of the field, which to day is, and to morrow is cast into the oven, shall he not much more clothe you, O ye of little faith? Therefore take no thought,*

*saying, What shall we eat? or, What shall we drink?
or, Wherewithal shall we be clothed? (For after all
these things do the Gentiles seek:) for your heavenly
Father knoweth that ye have need of all these things.
But seek ye first the kingdom of God, and his
righteousness; and all these things shall be added
unto you. Take therefore no thought for the morrow:
for the morrow shall take thought for the things of
itself. Sufficient unto the day is the evil thereof.
(Matthew 6:25-34)*

Fear focuses on the future--whether it is tomorrow, later this
week, or five years from now. Jesus said not to focus on or
worry about the future.

Fear leads to sin. Abraham was so afraid of Abimelech that
he lied, claiming that his wife, Sarah, was his sister (Genesis
20:1-13). Abraham's son, Isaac, also feared for his life for the
same reason and committed the same sin (Genesis 26:7). Ten
of the twelve spies who investigated the promised land were
terrified of the giants and their fears resulted in Israel's
disobedience and the death of a whole generation (Numbers
13). Saul tried to murder David because he feared him (1
Samuel 18:12,15,29) and later sinned by offering a burnt
offering because he feared his people would scatter (1 Samuel
13:11-12). This act cost Saul the kingdom.

What will fear cost you?

Spiritual Paralysis

The "fight or flight" response that is common to all people is
not the fear spoken of in this passage. "Fight or flight" is a
normal response that protects you in the face of perceived
danger. For example, if you are threatened by a dangerous
beast your "fight or flight" response kicks in so you can either

escape or protect yourself from the animal. This is a rational response to actual danger.

Psalm 91:5 is speaking of a paralyzing fear that causes you to procrastinate or refuse to act because you are fearful. It is a fear that can hinder you from fulfilling your divine destiny, as illustrated in this parable spoken by Jesus:

For the kingdom of heaven is as a man travelling into a far country, who called his own servants, and delivered unto them his goods. And unto one he gave five talents, to another two, and to another one; to every man according to his several ability; and straightway took his journey. Then he that had received the five talents went and traded with the same, and made them other five talents. And likewise he that had received two, he also gained other two. But he that had received one went and digged in the earth, and hid his lord's money. After a long time the lord of those servants cometh, and reckoneth with them. And so he that had received five talents came and brought other five talents, saying, Lord, thou deliveredst unto me five talents: behold, I have gained beside them five talents more. His lord said unto him, Well done, thou good and faithful servant: thou hast been faithful over a few things, I will make thee ruler over many things: enter thou into the joy of thy lord. He also that had received two talents came and said, Lord, thou deliveredst unto me two talents: behold, I have gained two other talents beside them. His lord said unto him, Well done, good and faithful servant; thou hast been faithful over a few things, I will make thee ruler over many things: enter thou into the joy of thy lord. Then he which had received the one talent came and said, Lord, I knew thee that thou art an hard man, reaping where thou hast not sown, and gathering where thou hast not strawed: And I was afraid, and went and hid thy talent in the earth: lo, there thou hast that is thine. His lord answered and said unto him, Thou wicked and slothful servant, thou knewest that I reap where I sowed not, and gather where I have not strawed: Thou oughtest therefore to have put my money to the exchangers, and then at my coming I should have received mine own with usury. Take therefore the talent from him, and give it unto him which hath ten talents. (Matthew 25:14-28)

Because of fear, the unfaithful servant did not use the talent which he had been given. What gifts, talents, or abilities have you been entrusted with that you have failed to use because you feared to do so?

You make decisions based on positive or negative emotions. Positive emotions stem from faith and help you make good decisions. Negative emotions result in bad decisions. Fear is a negative emotion that always results in poor decisions because it is the opposite of faith, and the Bible says that whatever is not of faith is sin (Romans 14:23).

Four Specific Dangers

Four specific dangers that you need not fear are mentioned in Psalm 91:5-6. These are terrors, arrows, pestilence, and destruction: *"You shall not be afraid of the terror by night, Nor of the arrow that flies by day, Nor of the pestilence that walks in darkness, Nor of the destruction that lays waste at noonday" (NKJV)*.

You learned at the beginning of this study that Psalm 91 is a spiritual revelation, so these fearful foes must be confronted spiritually. Every potential fear is represented by these four categories of terror, arrows, pestilence, and destruction.

Terror: The word "terror" refers to acts of violence and destruction, something terrible that causes you to fear. "Terrorism" and "terrorists"--two common words in our present troubled society--are derivatives of this word.

Psalm 91:5 says that we need not fear the terror by night, revealing that attacks of terrorism--both in the natural and spiritual worlds--are often cloaked in darkness. In the natural world, such attacks are frequently carried out under the canopy of the actual darkness of night. Spiritual darkness is also a breeding ground for terror. Israel was warned that if they did not obey God's commands then they would be victims of terror because they would be walking in spiritual darkness (Leviticus 26).

The Prophet Isaiah declared that those who are established in righteousness need not fear terror:

> *In righteousness shalt thou be established: thou shalt be far from oppression; for thou shalt not fear: and from terror; for it shall not come near thee.*
> *(Isaiah 54:14)*

Again, this does not mean that you might not experience an act of terror, but that you need not fear it. The Apostle Peter declared that even if you are called upon to suffer for righteousness sake, you need not be terrified:

> *But and if ye suffer for righteousness' sake, happy are ye: and be not afraid of their terror, neither be troubled; But sanctify the Lord God in your hearts: and be ready always to give an answer to every man that asketh you a reason of the hope that is in you with meekness and fear: Having a good conscience; that, whereas they speak evil of you, as of evildoers, they may be ashamed that falsely accuse your good*

conversation in Christ. For it is better, if the will of God be so, that ye suffer for well doing, than for evil doing. (1 Peter 3:14-17)

You may confront terror, but you need not fear because God is with you. How can you be assured of this? By continuing to follow in His shadow!

Arrows: An arrow is a long shaft with a sharp point on it which is normally shot from a bow. If you are struck by an arrow, it can be quite painful or even lethal. The Amplified Version of the Bible renders the word "arrow" as *"the evil plots and slander of the wicked."*

You may not be dodging actual arrows today unless you are out on an archery shooting range, but spiritually "arrows" can refer to harmful words:

> *Their tongue is as an arrow shot out; it speaketh deceit: one speaketh peaceably to his neighbour with his mouth, but in heart he layeth his wait.*
> *(Jeremiah 9:8)*

Negative words and evil plots can wound and destroy, but the Prophet Isaiah declared:

> *No weapon that is formed against thee shall prosper; and every tongue that shall rise against thee in judgment thou shalt condemn. This is the heritage of the servants of the Lord, and their righteousness is of me, saith the Lord. (Isaiah 54:17)*

This passage does not say that no weapons will be formed against you. It says those formed against you will not prosper. The word "prosper" means "final and complete success." It might seem that negative words, evil plots, or weapons have

100

prevailed, but these things cannot penetrate your secret place unless you allow them to do so.

There is no reason to fear the "arrows" of wicked--their evil plots and words. As a servant of God, dwelling in the secret place and abiding in His shadow, every weapon and every tongue that comes against you shall not prosper! Your spiritual shield of faith will protect you from all the fiery arrows launched by the enemy (Ephesians 6:16).

Pestilence: Pestilence refers to deadly infections or plagues and the word is used consistently in the Bible in relation to judgment sent from God for sin. Pestilence functions in darkness. You can't see it and you don't know it is there, but God does.

As a believer, you need not fear pestilence because--as you will learn when you study Psalm 91:8--you will only be a spectator and not a recipient of God's judgment. No pestilence sent from God will affect you when you remain in your secret place.

If you, as a believer, experience something that is perceived to be a pestilence, you can be assured it is not from God. It is the enemy that comes to kill, steal, and destroy (John 10:10). When the enemy attacks, God is not caught unawares and He eventually provides deliverance (Job 1-2, 42).

Destruction: The word "destruction" means to "abolish, destroy, and pull down." God does not want you to fear the destruction that comes at noon time. In the natural world, noon is a time to relax and eat lunch and--in many nations--take a short rest before resuming the work day. Spiritually speaking, noon is a time when you are not expecting destruction to strike. The enemy is active around the clock, however, but Psalm 91:5 says, "Don't fear! "

One of the best ways to eliminate the fear of destruction is to avoid the things that cause it. According to the Bible, working iniquity results in destruction: *"The way of the Lord is strength to the upright: but destruction shall be to the workers of iniquity" (Proverbs 10:29).* Pride results in destruction: *"Pride goeth before destruction, and an haughty spirit before a fall" (Proverbs 16:18).*

An interesting verse regarding destruction is found in Proverbs 17:19 which states, *"...he that exalteth his gate seeketh destruction."* In Bible days in Palestine, the people built the doors of their courtyards and houses very low, not more than three feet high. This was done so that the enemy could not ride their horses into the courtyard and house and spoil their goods. The top part of the gate was open, like a French door, to enable observation of an intruder. A person who, through pride and ostentation, made a high elaborate gate, was actually exposing himself to destruction because he couldn't see what was happening in his courtyard. Applied spiritually, "exalting the gate" refers to proud, boastful, arrogant speaking that can provide access for the enemy to enter your life. The Bible reveals that your own mouth causes destruction:

> *A fool's mouth is his destruction, and his lips are the snare of his soul. (Proverbs 18:7)*

Walking your own way instead of abiding in God's shadow leads to destruction:

> *Enter ye in at the strait gate: for wide is the gate, and broad is the way, that leadeth to destruction, and many there be which go in thereat. (Matthew 7:13)*

Teaching false doctrine brings swift destruction:

*But there were false prophets also among the people,
even as there shall be false teachers among you, who
privily shall bring in damnable heresies, even denying
the Lord that bought them, and bring upon themselves
swift destruction. (2 Peter 2:1)*

The psalmist praises God...*"Who redeemeth thy life from
destruction; who crowneth thee with lovingkindness and
tender mercies" (Psalm 103:4)*. This verse, combined with
Psalm 91:5-6, confirms that you need not fear destruction
and that God stands ready to redeem you from it.

These four categories: Terror, arrows, pestilence, and
destruction--cover every kind of attack in the natural and
spiritual worlds that a believer might confront. In the face of
it all, God says, "Do not fear." You don't have to be afraid,
because you are walking in His shadow. You are not alone.
He is right there to deliver you from terror, arrows, pestilence,
and destruction.

Overcoming Fear

Fear does not come from God. The Bible is clear that...*"God
hath not given us the spirit of fear; but of power, and of love,
and of a sound mind" (2 Timothy 1:7)*. If fear does not come
from God, then it comes from your enemy, Satan. This verse
tells us that God's power, His love, and a sound mind
eliminate fear.

Power: Jesus said, *"Behold, I give unto you power to tread
on serpents and scorpions, and over all the power of the
enemy: and nothing shall by any means hurt you" (Luke
10:19)*. If you have power over all the power of the enemy
and nothing can hurt you, then you need not fear.

When the giant Goliath challenged the people of Israel, their experienced warriors were afraid of him and retreated (1 Samuel 17:24). So how did the young shepherd boy, David, face the giant without fear? David saw God as bigger than the giant, greater than his own fear:

> *Then said David to the Philistine, Thou comest to me with a sword, and with a spear, and with a shield: but I come to thee in the name of the Lord of hosts, the God of the armies of Israel, whom thou hast defied. This day will the Lord deliver thee into mine hand; and I will smite thee, and take thine head from thee; and I will give the carcases of the host of the Philistines this day unto the fowls of the air, and to the wild beasts of the earth; that all the earth may know that there is a God in Israel. And all this assembly shall know that the Lord saveth not with sword and spear: for the battle is the Lord's, and he will give you into our hands. (1 Samuel 17:45-47)*

Instead of retreating in fear, David rushed forward and conquered the giant.

Don't play the "what if?" game. "What if this happens, what if that happens?" The power to face difficult situations is given when it is needed, not when you are worrying over the future:

> *For we have not an high priest which cannot be touched with the feeling of our infirmities; but was in all points tempted like as we are, yet without sin. Let us therefore come boldly unto the throne of grace, that we may obtain mercy, and find **grace to help in time of need.** (Hebrews 4:15-16)*

You have unlimited power through Jesus Christ. The Bible speaks of the power of the gospel, the power of the Holy Spirit, the power of love, the power of His resurrection, and the power of the Word of God. Later on in this study, you will also learn of the tremendous power you have though the names of God, Jesus, and the Holy Spirit.

You also have the power *to "Submit yourselves therefore to God. Resist the devil, and he will flee from you" (James 4:7).* When you submit to God and resist the devil, he will flee and take the spirit of fear along with him!

Love: Perfect love casts out fear:

> *And we have known and believed the love that God hath to us. God is love; and he that dwelleth in love dwelleth in God, and God in him. Herein is our love made perfect, that we may have boldness in the day of judgment: because as he is, so are we in this world. There is no fear in love; but perfect love casteth out fear: because fear hath torment. He that feareth is not made perfect in love. There is no fear in love; but perfect love casteth out fear: because fear hath torment. He that feareth is not made perfect in love. (1 John 4:16-18)*

When you really love someone, you trust them with your well-being and that eliminates fear. You can relax with them. You are at peace. You know they care for you and will do you no harm. You cannot love someone and fear them at the same time. When you really come to understand God's tremendous love for you, fear will be eliminated. You need not fear a God who loves you and with whom you dwell in the secret place.

When the Bible speaks of the fear of the Lord, it is not talking about being fearful of a demanding God. It is speaking of respecting and honoring a God who loves you:

> *Let those who fear the Lord say:"His love endures forever." In my anguish I cried to the Lord, and he answered by setting me free. The Lord is with me; I will not be afraid. What can man do to me?*
> *(Psalm 118:4-6, NIV)*

The opposite of fear is peace, which is a result of perfected love. Jesus said:

> *Peace I leave with you; My [own] peace I now give and bequeath to you. Not as the world gives do I give to you. Do not let your hearts be troubled, neither let them be afraid. [Stop allowing yourselves to be agitated and disturbed; and do not permit yourselves to be fearful and intimidated and cowardly and unsettled.] (John 14:27, AMP)*

Peace is a gift Jesus has made available to all true believers, but like any promise, you must claim it. The peace He gives passes human understanding:

> *And God's peace [shall be yours, that tranquil state of a soul assured of its salvation through Christ, and so fearing nothing from God and being content with its earthly lot of whatever sort that is, that peace] which transcends all understanding shall garrison and mount guard over your hearts and minds in Christ Jesus. (Philippians 4:7, AMP)*

The peace of God is beyond measure, unsurpassed and unequaled by any other peace. It is a peace that dispels all fear and is in a category all by itself.

You maintain your peace by casting all your care on God: *"Casting all your care upon him; for he careth for you" (1 Peter 5:7).* "Casting" means to hurl or throw violently with force and it indicates continuous action. "Care" means anxiety, trouble, affliction, and difficulties--anything that generates fear. You must continuously cast all of your fear-generating cares upon Jesus and...

> *Be careful for nothing; but in every thing by prayer and supplication with thanksgiving let your requests be made known unto God. And the peace of God, which passeth all understanding, shall keep your hearts and minds through Christ Jesus.*
> *(Philippians 4:6-7)*

When you are praying and worshiping God in your secret place, you will refuse to answer when fear knocks on the door of your heart and mind.

How is your love perfected? When you keep His Word: *"But whoso keepeth his word, in him verily is the love of God perfected: hereby know we that we are in him" (1 John 2:5).* By keeping God's Word, you not only know you are in Him, but you know that His love is perfected in you--which means fear must flee!

A sound mind: Irrational fear is just that: Not rational. It is the result of irrational thinking, so you cannot deal with fear by trying to be rational. You must develop a sound mind that cannot be tormented by fear. You do this by living under the control of the Spirit rather than the flesh:

For they that are after the flesh do mind the things of the flesh; but they that are after the Spirit the things of the Spirit. For to be carnally minded is death; but to be spiritually minded is life and peace. (Romans 8:5-6)

The carnality of the world results in fear. Being spiritually minded--focusing on God and eternal things--results in peace. If you are fearful, then you are not living life in the Spirit because the Spirit does not fear.

As you present yourself to God as a living sacrifice, your mind will be transformed:

I beseech you therefore, brethren, by the mercies of God, that ye present your bodies a living sacrifice, holy, acceptable unto God, which is your reasonable service. And be not conformed to this world: but be ye transformed by the renewing of your mind, that ye may prove what is that good, and acceptable, and perfect, will of God. (Romans 12:1-2)

You will either conform or be transformed. The less you conform to the world, the more your mind will be transformed and negative emotions such as fear will be eliminated. First Corinthians 2:16 assures that you can have the mind of Christ and Philippians 2:5 admonishes you to *"Let this mind be in you, which was also in Christ Jesus."* You have the ability to permit the same mind that Jesus had to be in you. It is your decision.

You can also conquer many fears by eliminating things that feed fear such as media violence in news reports, horror movies, and violent video games.

Perhaps your parents instilled fear in you or you received it through a generational spirit. You will recall that Isaac acted in fear just as his father, Abraham, did. He lied about his wife because he was fearful. Even statements made by your parents like "Be careful. You are going to fall!" can generate fear. Command generational spirits of fear and inherited tendencies to fear to go in the name of Jesus!

Many fears result from materialism, fearing that you will lose your money or possessions. Jesus said:

> *Lay not up for yourselves treasures upon earth, where moth and rust doth corrupt, and where thieves break through and steal: But lay up for yourselves treasures in heaven, where neither moth nor rust doth corrupt, and where thieves do not break through nor steal: For where your treasure is, there will your heart be also. (Matthew 6:19-21)*

Stop thinking about your bank accounts and material possessions. Keep your mind focused on things of eternal value and fear will leave!

Situations perceived as traumatic may also breed fear. Ask God to alleviate your fear and then take steps to deal with it. For example, a person who is afraid of heights should ask God to eliminate his concerns and then he might expose himself to ever increasing elevations in order to overcome his fear. Face your fear head-on and conquer it in the name of Jesus by both spiritual and practical strategies.

Phobias are irrational fears that affect your behavior. Because they are irrational, they cannot be dealt with through rational, natural means. That is why you must turn to the Lord to deal with your fears. David said, *"I sought the Lord, and he heard me, and delivered me from all my fears" (Psalm 34:4).*

Fear is a spirit generated by Satan and it begins in your mind. That is why you must learn to successfully fight the battle for your mind:

> *For the weapons of our warfare are not carnal, but mighty through God to the pulling down of strong holds; casting down imaginations, and every high thing that exalteth itself against the knowledge of God, and bringing into captivity every thought to the obedience of Christ...(2 Corinthians 10:4-5)*

Fear is a battle that starts with lies instigated by the father of lies, Satan (John 8:44). This is why the scriptures direct you to cast down vain imaginations. Cast down means to conquer, pull down, and to hold under one's power. The word "imaginations" means logic. Your mind can develop strongholds that result from logical reasoning. A sound mind is one controlled by the Holy Spirit, rather than the logic of your own carnal mind.

In order to conquer fear, you must acknowledge it, refuse to retreat from it, and do what you can in both the natural and spiritual worlds to face fear head-on with the assurance of Psalm 91:5 that you need not fear.

Why Are You So Fearful?

Whatever the reasons for your fear, Christ's question to you is the same as to His disciples one stormy night on the Sea of Galilee: *"Why are you so fearful? How is it that you have no faith?" (Mark 4:40).*

If you are bound by fear, think about the Lord's question. Why are you so fearful? When you are exhibiting fear, you are not demonstrating faith. Faith comes by hearing the Word of God and applying it in your life. Get into the Word of God to strengthen your faith. Make a list of all the "fear nots" in the Bible and apply them to your life. There are hundreds of these verses, because God knew that we would wrestle continuously with this tormenting spirit.

As you conclude this chapter, make this powerful declaration penned by the psalmist under the inspiration of the Holy Spirit:

> *What time I am afraid, I will trust in thee...In God I have put my trust; I will not fear what flesh can do unto me...In God have I put my trust: I will not be afraid what man can do unto me. (Psalms 56:3-4)*

Chapter Nine
Standing Strong

"A thousand may fall at your side,
and ten thousand at your right hand;
but it shall not come near you."

When people start falling all around you, do not become frightened and assume it will happen to you. Psalm 91:7 declares that although a thousand--or even ten thousand--fall around you, you do not have to fall.

The New American Standard version states *"it shall not approach you"*. The New Living Translation says *"...these evils will not touch you"*. The Message Bible declares *"Even though others succumb all around, drop like flies right and left, no harm will even graze you. You'll stand untouched, watch it all from a distance."* The Wycliff Bible says the evil will *"not even come close to you".*

The word "thousand" used in this passage means an infinite number in Hebrew. So the passage is actually saying that even if an infinite number--or ten thousand times infinity-- should fall around you, you can remain standing.

Again, remember that this promise is to those dwelling in the secret place and abiding in the shadow of Almighty God. You must continually return to the premise of this passage in Psalm 91:1, because it is the foundational truth upon which all of these promises are based.

The Prophet Isaiah admonished:

*Thus saith the Lord, Stand ye in the ways, and see,
and ask for the old paths, where is the good way, and
walk therein, and ye shall find rest for your souls. But
they said, We will not walk therein. (Jeremiah 6:16)*

If you seek for the tried and true path--the good way--you will
find it in the shadow of the Almighty. It is by remaining
there that you will be secure from falling.

The Causes Of Falls

People fall in the natural world because of obstacles and
imbalance. That is pretty much true in the spiritual world
also. If you are following in the shadow of Almighty God,
He will remove the obstacles in your way. If His truth is your
shield, you will not become a target for deception. You can
stand secure in your relationship with God and, even though a
thousand may fall at your side and ten thousand at your right
hand, it will not affect you.

People wonder how great men and women can fall into sin
when they have apparently known God intimately and
ministered effectively for Him. The answer is simple:
Anyone is capable of falling if they abandon their secret place
and stop walking in God's shadow. When you go your own
way, do your own thing, and your time for intimate
fellowship with God is crowded out--even by ministry--that is
when you get into trouble.

A survey of the Bible, as well as the accounts of modern day
believers who have fallen into sin, reveals that spiritual falls
are usually caused by one or more of five major factors:
Pride, power, people, prosperity, and problems. Let's look at
examples of each drawn from the Bible because *"...all these
things happened unto them for ensamples: and they are
written for our admonition, upon whom the ends of the world*

are come. Wherefore let him that thinketh he standeth take heed lest he fall." (1 Corinthians 10:11-12).

Although these are major factors that have been identified as leading to spiritual falls, each person is responsible for their own failures. If you are tempted by pride, power, people, prosperity, or problems, then remember this warning:

> *Let no man say when he is tempted, I am tempted of God: for God cannot be tempted with evil, neither tempteth he any man: But every man is tempted, when he is drawn away of his own lust, and enticed. Then when lust hath conceived it bringeth forth sin: and sin, when it is finished, bringeth forth death. (James 1:13-15)*

This is why the Apostle Paul warns believers not to be ignorant of Satan's schemes (2 Corinthians 2:11). It is the choice you make when faced with temptation that determines whether you fall or emerge victorious.

Pride. Pride has been a major factor in spiritual falls down through the centuries. One prime example is the story of King Nebuchadnezzar in Daniel chapter 4. This king proudly boasted, *"Is not this great Babylon, that I have built for the house of the kingdom by the might of my power, and for the honour of my majesty?" (Daniel 4:30).* In the very hour he made this boastful statement:

> *While the word was in the king's mouth, there fell a voice from heaven, saying, O king Nebuchadnezzar, to thee it is spoken; The kingdom is departed from thee. And they shall drive thee from men, and thy dwelling shall be with the beasts of the field: they shall make thee to eat grass as oxen, and seven times shall pass over thee, until thou know that the most*

High ruleth in the kingdom of men, and giveth it to whomsoever he will. The same hour was the thing fulfilled upon Nebuchadnezzar: and he was driven from men, and did eat grass as oxen, and his body was wet with the dew of heaven, till his hairs were grown like eagles' feathers, and his nails like birds' claws. (Daniel 4:31-33)

The prophet Daniel comments further concerning the fall of Nebuchadnezzar:

But when his heart was lifted up, and his mind hardened in pride, he was deposed from his kingly throne, and they took his glory from him: And he was driven from the sons of men; and his heart was made like the beasts, and his dwelling was with the wild asses: they fed him with grass like oxen, and his body was wet with the dew of heaven; till he knew that the most high God ruled in the kingdom of men, and that he appointeth over it whomsoever he will.
(Daniel 5:20-21)

Fortunately, King Nebuchadnezzar learned his lesson. Here is his testimony:

And at the end of the days I Nebuchadnezzar lifted up mine eyes unto heaven, and mine understanding returned unto me, and I blessed the most High, and I praised and honoured him that liveth for ever, whose dominion is an everlasting dominion, and his kingdom is from generation to generation: And all the inhabitants of the earth are reputed as nothing: and he doeth according to his will in the army of heaven, and among the inhabitants of the earth: and none can stay his hand, or say unto him, What doest thou? At the same time my reason returned unto me; and for

*the glory of my kingdom, mine honour and brightness
returned unto me; and my counsellors and my lords
sought unto me; and I was established in my kingdom,
and excellent majesty was added unto me. Now I
Nebuchadnezzar praise and extol and honour the
King of heaven, all whose works are truth, and his
ways judgment: and those that walk in pride he is
able to abase. (Daniel 4:34-37)*

The Bible is clear about the relation between pride and
spiritual falls: *"Pride goeth before destruction, and an
haughty spirit before a fall" (Proverbs 16:18).* That's pretty
clear, isn't it?

Pride was manifested in Lucifer's sinful desire to be God and
was evident in the first sin when Eve wanted to be like God
and know all things. This is why *"Every one that is proud in
heart is an abomination to the Lord" (Proverbs 16:5)* and
pride is one of the things God hates most (Proverbs 6:17).
You cannot retain a prideful attitude and remain in the secret
place under the shadow of the Almighty. Confess pride and
get rid of it before it causes you to fall.

Power: Power is another major cause of spiritual falls.
Samson was the most powerful man to ever live. As long as
he served God, his physical strength was unchallenged.
Because he was so powerful, he began to think he could do as
he pleased--a mistake many people make. Power and its
accompanying prestige and position often make a person
think that they are above the laws of God.

Samson thought he could violate God's law by committing
immorality with a harlot (Judges 16:1). He began to treat his
God-given power lightly, first claiming if he was bound with
green cords or a new rope, he would not be able to escape.
His next claim was that if the hairs of his head were woven

into several strands he would be like other men. He was fooling around with the power of God, something that was so great, so special, and so divine that it should have been highly valued and not taken lightly.

Thinking he was too powerful to fall, Samson finally told the evil Delilah that the true secret of his strength was in his hair and if it was cut he would be as other men. While Samson was sleeping, Delilah cut his hair. Then she awoke him...

> *And she said, "The Philistines are upon you, Samson!" So he awoke from his sleep, and said, "I will go out as before, at other times, and shake myself free!" But he did not know that the Lord had departed from him. Then the Philistines took him and put out his eyes, and brought him down to Gaza. They bound him with bronze fetters, and he became a grinder in the prison. (Judges 16:20-21, NKJV)*

Under God's anointing, Samson had ripped gates from the walls of the city and killed a thousand Philistines with the jawbone of a donkey. He thought he was so powerful that he could do as he pleased and violate God's laws, but he was stripped of his strength and fell into the hands of the enemy. One of the saddest phrases in the Bible is *"...he did not know that the Lord had departed from him."* Samson didn't even miss the Lord, because he hadn't been living in the Shadow of the Almighty. He had been spending time in the enemy's territory.

People: Have you ever tripped over someone in the natural world? Or perhaps someone pushed you and caused you to fall? The same is possible in the spiritual world. Solomon, the wisest man who ever lived, began his downward spiral when he made alliances with evil kings and became intimate with ungodly women.

This is why the scriptures warn: *"He that walketh with wise men shall be wise: but a companion of fools shall be destroyed" (Proverbs 13:20).* The Word also warns, *"Make no friendship with an angry man; and with a furious man thou shalt not go: Lest thou learn his ways, and get a snare to thy soul" (Proverbs 22:24-25).*

Substitute any negative word for the word "angry" and the premise remains true. If you are close friends with a bitter man, you will learn his ways. If you hang out with alcoholics, don't be surprised if you are enticed to drink--"just one!" If you are addicted to drugs, your addiction most likely started when someone introduced you to narcotics and showed you how to use them.

A classic example of how people can be used by the enemy to cause another person to fall is that of an unnamed prophet of God whose story is recorded in 1 Kings chapter 13. God sent this man to Bethel to deliver a message to King Jeroboam. God specifically commanded this prophet not to tarry there and told him not to eat or drink anything. The unnamed prophet faithfully delivered God's message and was on his way back home when he encountered a man who said...

> *...I am a prophet also as thou art; and an angel spake unto me by the word of the Lord, saying, Bring him back with thee into thine house, that he may eat bread and drink water. But he lied unto him.*
> *(I Kings 13:18)*

Instead of obeying the Lord, the unnamed prophet went to the so-called prophet's house. He tarried there and ate and drank with his host, and because he did so in violation to God's instructions, he died in a lion attack on his way home.

Be careful that you do not cause another person to fall. The Apostle Paul said, *"Let...no man put a stumbling block or an occasion to fall in his brother's way" (Romans 14:13).*

Prosperity. Material blessings and success can also result in spiritual falls. God warned the Israelites regarding the pitfalls of prosperity prior to their entry into their promised land:

> *And it shall be, when the Lord thy God shall have brought thee into the land which he sware unto thy fathers, to Abraham, to Isaac, and to Jacob, to give thee great and goodly cities, which thou buildedst not, And houses full of all good things, which thou filledst not, and wells digged, which thou diggedst not, vineyards and olive trees, which thou plantedst not; when thou shalt have eaten and be full; Then beware lest thou forget the Lord, which brought thee forth out of the land of Egypt, from the house of bondage. (Deuteronomy 6:10-12)*

The historical record in the Bible reveals that Israel did not heed this warning. Years later, the prophet Hosea declared concerning them:

> *Israel is a luxuriant vine that puts forth its [material] fruit. According to the abundance of his fruit he has multiplied his altars [to idols]; according to the goodness and prosperity of their land they have made goodly pillars or obelisks [to false gods]. Their heart is divided and deceitful; now shall they be found guilty and suffer punishment. The Lord will smite and break down [the horns of] their altars; He will destroy their [idolatrous] pillars.*
> *(Hosea 10:1-2, AMP)*

When Israel experienced material blessings and prosperity in

120

their new land, they turned away from God.

The Bible warns against trusting in riches: *"He that trusteth in his riches shall fall: but the righteous shall flourish as a branch" (Proverbs 11:28).* Prosperity leads to believing that since you are prosperous, you must be blessed by God despite the fact you are sinning. You begin to think that you are above falling. This leads to a wrong assumption like David once made (and from which he repented) when he said in his prosperity, *"I shall never be moved" (Psalm 30:6).*

The Apostle Paul warned:

> *But they that will be rich fall into temptation and a snare, and into many foolish and hurtful lusts, which drown men in destruction and perdition. For the love of money is the root of all evil: which while some coveted after, they have erred from the faith, and pierced themselves through with many sorrows.*
> *(1 Timothy 6:9-10)*

It is not money itself that is wrong, but the love of money which leads to selfishness, greed, and abandoning your relationship with God.

Problems. From the time the nation of Israel left Egypt, they did not handle their problems properly. They complained about not having water (Exodus 17:2). They didn't appreciate the manna God sent them (Numbers 11:7-8). Despite the fact they had been slaves, they were ready to go back to Egypt because they were hungry for the food there (Numbers 11:5). When they thought Moses had abandoned them due to his long stay in the mountains, they created and worshipped an idol (Exodus 32:1-8). In times of difficulty, the Israelites also criticized their leadership (Numbers 16).

Problems either turn you to God or away from Him. Israel was continually falling into sin because they did not know how to handle problems properly and it was this same issue that prevented them from entering the promised land. All they saw were giants instead of the blessings that had been reserved for them. Because of their refusal to enter the promised land, an entire generation died in the wilderness.

Many people fall spiritually when they cannot deal properly with life's problems. Jesus warned about this in the parable of the farmer sowing seed which represented God's Word:

> *But he that received the seed into stony places, the same is he that heareth the word, and anon with joy receiveth it; Yet hath he not root in himself, but dureth for a while: for when tribulation or persecution ariseth because of the word, by and by he is offended. (Matthew 13:20-21)*

Through your study of Psalm 91, the seed of God's Word is taking root in your heart. Do not let the problems of life cause you to be offended at God and fall away from your faith.

Recovering From A Fall

Spiritual falls are usually caused by issues relating to pride, power, people, prosperity, or problems, As you have studied this chapter, you may have recognized the cause of your own spiritual fall or areas where you are in danger of falling. If so, review these directives given to the church at Ephesus:

> *Unto the angel of the church of Ephesus write; These things saith he that holdeth the seven stars in his right hand, who walketh in the midst of the seven golden candlesticks; I know thy works, and thy labour, and thy patience, and how thou canst not bear them which*

are evil: and thou hast tried them which say they are
apostles, and are not, and hast found them liars: And
hast borne, and hast patience, and for my name's sake
hast laboured, and hast not fainted. Nevertheless I
have somewhat against thee, because thou hast left
thy first love. Remember therefore from whence thou
art fallen, and repent, and do the first works...
(Revelation 2:1-5)

The believers at Ephesus were great workers for God. They
were patient and abhorred evil, but they had fallen away from
their first love. God directs them to remember from where
they had fallen, repent, and do their first works again.

If you have fallen or are in danger of falling, ask God for
forgiveness and then do your first works again. The first
works include the basics of prayer, worship, and study of the
Word that will rekindle your passion for living in the secret
place. In the natural world, many falls are caused by
weakness because of inadequate food or dehydration due to
lack of water. Jesus is the bread and water of life. Get back
into God's presence and into His Word and you will regain
the spiritual strength to stand strong.

God doesn't want more service from you. He wants you to
repent and remember from where you have fallen. The
Prophet Hosea admonished God's people:

O Israel, return unto the Lord thy God; for thou hast
fallen by thine iniquity. Take with you words, and turn
to the Lord: say unto him, Take away all iniquity, and
receive us graciously: so will we render the calves of
our lips. (Hosea 14:1-2)

Because of your fall, you may feel hopeless, alone, and
abandoned, but Jesus said:

Are not two sparrows sold for a farthing? and one of them shall not fall on the ground without your Father. But the very hairs of your head are all numbered. Fear ye not therefore, ye are of more value than many sparrows. (Matthew 10:29-31)

God sees when a sparrow falls. You are of much more value and He knows exactly where you are, what caused your fall, and He longs to help you get back up again.

The good news is that if you have fallen, the Lord will lift you up again if you will repent. The Bible says that *"The Lord upholdeth all that fall, and raiseth up all those that be bowed down" (Psalm 145:14).* The psalmist declares:

The steps of a good man are ordered by the Lord: and he delighteth in his way. Though he fall, he shall not be utterly cast down: for the Lord upholdeth him with his hand. (Psalm 37:23-24)

...And an old Japanese proverb says, "Fall seven times. Stand up eight."

The Prophet Isaiah declared:

Hast thou not known? hast thou not heard, that the everlasting God, the Lord, the Creator of the ends of the earth, fainteth not, neither is weary? there is no searching of his understanding. He giveth power to the faint; and to them that have no might he increaseth strength. Even the youths shall faint and be weary, and the young men shall utterly fall: But they that wait upon the Lord shall renew their strength; they shall mount up with wings as eagles; they shall

*run, and not be weary; and they shall walk, and not
faint. (Isaiah 40:28-31)*

Even if you have "utterly fallen" as mentioned in this passage, you can renew your strength by returning to the secret place and waiting before God. You can rise up, walk without fainting, and run without growing weary. You can once again stand strong in the Lord.

Standing Strong

God wants your Christian experience to be one of going from strength to strength, not from failure to failure (Psalm 84:7). You can stand against the wiles of the devil and withstand evil by appropriating your spiritual armor which is detailed in Ephesians 6:11-17. The Bible says having done all to stand, then stand--meaning hold your ground!

> *Be prepared. You're up against far more than you can
> handle on your own. Take all the help you can get,
> every weapon God has issued, so that when it's all
> over but the shouting you'll still be on your feet.
> (Ephesians 6:13, MSG).*

The Word admonishes us to *"...be strong in the Lord, and in the power of his might' (Ephesians 6:10).* The word "strong" means "explosive strength and ability, excessive manifested strength." It is from a Greek word *dunamis* from which we get the word dynamite. It is not just intellectual power, it is manifested power!

The power of His might is the power of the Holy Spirit within you. It is the same power that raised Jesus Christ from the dead (Romans 8:11) and it is a power that is greater than all the power of the enemy (1 John 4:4). The word "might" conveys the image of an extremely strong man. You have the strength, power, and might of Almighty God within you. How can you not remain standing? Here are some biblical guidelines to keep you from falling and help you stand strong in the Lord:

Abide in the Lord: *...Stand fast in the Lord.*
(Philippians 4:1)

Establish your life on the Word of God: *The grass withereth, the flower fadeth: but the word of our God shall stand for ever. (Isaiah 40:8)*

Rely on God's grace: *By whom also we have access by faith into this grace wherein we stand, and rejoice in hope of the glory of God. (Romans 5:2)*

Put your faith in God's power: *That your faith should not stand in the wisdom of men, but in the power of God.*
(1 Corinthians 2:5)

Stand in the power of the gospel: *Moreover, brethren, I declare unto you the gospel which I preached unto you, which also ye have received, and wherein ye stand...*
(1 Corinthians 15:1)

Have faith in God: *Not for that we have dominion over your faith, but are helpers of your joy: for by faith ye stand.*
(2 Corinthians 1:24)

Remain free from bondage: *Stand fast therefore in the liberty wherewith Christ hath made us free, and be not entangled again with the yoke of bondage. (Galatians 5:1)*

Listen to Godly counselors: *Where no counsel is, the people fall: but in the multitude of counsellors there is safety.*
(Proverbs 11:14)

Equip yourself with spiritual armor: *Put on the whole armour of God, that ye may be able to stand against the wiles of the devil. Wherefore take unto you the whole armour of God, that ye may be able to withstand in the evil day, and having done all, to stand. Stand therefore, having your loins girt about with truth, and having on the breastplate of righteousness. (Ephesians 6:11,13-14)*

Do God's will: *...that ye may stand perfect and complete in all the will of God. (Colossians 4:12)*

Obey God's Word: *Therefore shall ye keep all the commandments which I command you this day, that ye may be strong, and go in and possess the land, whither ye go to possess it... (Deuteronomy 11:8)*

Seek God's strength: *Seek the Lord and his strength, seek his face continually. (1 Chronicles 16:11).*

Allow God's strength to be manifested in your weakness: *And he said unto me, My grace is sufficient for thee: for my strength is made perfect in weakness. Most gladly therefore will I rather glory in my infirmities, that the power of Christ may rest upon me. (2 Corinthians 12:9)*

Confess the Lord as your strength to stand: Here are some biblical confessions to make regarding your spiritual strength:

The Lord is my strength and song, and he is become my salvation: he is my God, and I will prepare him an habitation; my father's God, and I will exalt him. (Exodus 15:2)

God is my strength and power: and he maketh my way perfect. (2 Samuel 22:33)

For thou hast girded me with strength to battle...
(2 Samuel 22:40 and Psalms 18:39)

The Lord is my rock, and my fortress, and my deliverer; my God, my strength, in whom I will trust; my buckler, and the horn of my salvation, and my high tower. (Psalms 18:2)

It is God that girdeth me with strength, and maketh my way perfect. (Psalms 18:32)

...The Lord is my light and my salvation; whom shall I fear? the Lord is the strength of my life; of whom shall I be afraid? (Psalms 27:1)

The Lord is my strength and my shield; my heart trusted in him, and I am helped: therefore my heart greatly rejoiceth; and with my song will I praise him. (Psalms 28:7)

...God is our refuge and strength, a very present help in trouble. (Psalms 46:1)

I will go in the strength of the Lord God: I will make mention of thy righteousness, even of thine only. (Psalms 71:16)

O God the Lord, the strength of my salvation, thou hast covered my head in the day of battle. (Psalms 140:7)

Behold, God is my salvation; I will trust, and not be afraid: for the Lord Jehovah is my strength and my song; he also is become my salvation. (Isaiah 12:2)

The Lord God is my strength, and he will make my feet like hinds' feet, and he will make me to walk upon mine high places. To the chief singer on my stringed instruments. (Habakkuk 3:19)

You Will Never Fall

Is there any way to insure that you will never fall spiritually? The Scripture says yes! The Apostle Peter details exactly how to do this:

> *According as his divine power hath given unto us all things that pertain unto life and godliness, through the knowledge of him that hath called us to glory and virtue: Whereby are given unto us exceeding great and precious promises: that by these ye might be partakers of the divine nature, having escaped the corruption that is in the world through lust. And beside this, giving all diligence, add to your faith virtue; and to virtue knowledge; And to knowledge temperance; and to temperance patience; and to patience godliness; And to godliness brotherly kindness; and to brotherly kindness charity. For if these things be in you, and abound, they make you that ye shall neither be barren nor unfruitful in the knowledge of our Lord Jesus Christ. But he that lacketh these things is blind, and cannot see afar off, and hath forgotten that he was purged from his old sins. Wherefore the rather, brethren, give diligence to make your calling and election sure: for if ye do these things, **ye shall never fall**: For so an entrance shall be ministered unto you abundantly into the everlasting kingdom of our Lord and Saviour Jesus Christ. (2 Peter 1:3-11)*

Peter says if you do these things, you will never fall. What things is he referring to? The things he discussed in the preceding passage. God has already given you all things that are necessary to live a godly life. You have His promises, you are partakers of His divine nature, and He has redeemed you from the world. You have faith and He wants to add to your faith virtue, knowledge, temperance, patience, godliness, brotherly kindness, and charity. The promise is that if you do these things, you will not only have a fruitful life and ministry, but you will never fall!

What better way to end this chapter than with the great benediction from the book of Jude: *"Now unto him that is able to keep you from falling, and to present you faultless before the presence of his glory with exceeding joy, To the only wise God our Saviour, be glory and majesty, dominion and power, both now and ever. Amen" (Jude 24-25).*

SECTION THREE
DIVINE PRESERVATION

"Only with your eyes shall you look
and see the reward of the wicked.
Because you have made the Lord,
which is my refuge, even the most High,
your dwelling place;
There shall no evil befall you,
nor shall any plague
come near your dwelling."

(Psalm 91:8-10)

Chapter Ten
Escaping The Reward Of The Wicked

"Only with your eyes shall you look,
and see the reward of the wicked."

Psalm 91:8 reveals that God will someday deal with the wicked, but as believers we will only witness His judgment, not be recipients of it. Believers will stand before God with the imputed righteousness of Jesus Christ resting upon them because of their decision to accept His sacrifice for their sin.

As we see the evil in the world around us and as that evil sometimes touches us and the lives of those we love, we wonder when justice will prevail. We witness courts and judges making poor decisions. We watch as criminals are set free because of technicalities in the legal system. We see innocent people incarcerated. Solomon expressed similar concerns when he noted:

> *And moreover I saw under the sun the place of judgment, that wickedness was there; and the place of righteousness, that iniquity was there. I said in mine heart, God shall judge the righteous and the wicked: for there is a time there for every purpose and for every work. (Ecclesiastes 3:16-17)*

Solomon saw that iniquity often went unpunished, but he realized that although delayed, fair and righteous judgment would eventually come. The Prophet Habakkuk expressed similar concern when he penned these words:

> *O Lord, how long shall I cry, and thou wilt not hear! even cry out unto thee of violence, and thou wilt not save!...Therefore the law is slacked, and judgment*

doth never go forth: for the wicked doth compass about the righteous; therefore wrong judgment proceedeth...Thou art of purer eyes than to behold evil, and canst not look on iniquity: wherefore lookest thou upon them that deal treacherously, and holdest thy tongue when the wicked devoureth the man that is more righteous than he? (Habakkuk 1:2,4,13)

The Prophet Jeremiah prayed:

Righteous art thou, O Lord, when I plead with thee: yet let me talk with thee of thy judgments: Wherefore doth the way of the wicked prosper? Wherefore are all they happy that deal very treacherously? (Jeremiah 12:1)

David was also troubled by the seeming lack of judgment upon the wicked and he questioned, *"O God, how long shall the adversary reproach? Shall the enemy blaspheme thy name for ever?" (Psalm 74:10).* He asked God to...

Keep not thou silence...hold not thy peace, and be not still, O God. For, lo, thine enemies make a tumult: and they that hate thee have lifted up the head. They have taken crafty counsel against thy people, and consulted against thy hidden ones. (Psalm 83:1-3)

David fretted over the wicked until he considered their future. Then he declared:

Fret not thyself because of evildoers, neither be thou envious against the workers of iniquity. For they shall soon be cut down like the grass, and wither as the green herb...Rest in the Lord, and wait patiently for him: fret not thyself because of him who prospereth in his way, because of the man who bringeth wicked

devices to pass...Cease from anger, and forsake wrath: fret not thyself in any wise to do evil. For evildoers shall be cut off: but those that wait upon the Lord, they shall inherit the earth...For yet a little while, and the wicked shall not be: yea, thou shalt diligently consider his place, and it shall not be. I have seen the wicked in great power, and spreading himself like a green bay tree. Yet he passed away, and, lo, he was not: yea, I sought him, but he could not be found...the wicked shall be cut off.
(Portions of Psalm 37)

In Psalm 91:8, God assures those who abide in the secret place that not only will the unrepentant wicked be appropriately rewarded for evil, but believers will witness their judgment. It will be much like when the Israelites saw the Egyptians perish in the Red Sea and wash up dead on the seashore (Exodus 14).

The Amplified Bible declares, *"Only a spectator shall you be [yourself inaccessible in the secret place of the Most High] as you witness the reward of the wicked."* The Holman Bible promises you will only *"...witness the punishment of the wicked".* The New International Readers Version says *"...you will see with your own eyes how God punishes sinful people".* The Wycliff Bible explains *"Nevertheless thou shalt see with thine eyes; yea, thou shalt see the punishment of the sinners".*

Escaping The Reward

Prior to the outpouring of God's wrath on earth, Jesus will return for believers in what has come to be called the rapture. The word "rapture" is actually not used in the original manuscripts of the Bible, but is a term that is commonly applied to the return of Jesus Christ to catch away true believers from earth. The Bible teaches that the Lord will return for believers in the same manner that He departed:

> *And when he (Jesus) had spoken these things, while they beheld, he was taken up; and a cloud received him out of their sight. And while they looked stedfastly toward heaven as he went up, behold, two men stood by them in white apparel; Which also said, Ye men of Galilee, why stand ye gazing up into heaven? This same Jesus, which is taken up from you into heaven, shall so come in like manner as ye have seen him go into heaven. (Acts 1:9-11)*

Jesus promised His followers:

> *...I go to prepare a place for you. And if I go and prepare a place for you, I will come again and receive you unto myself; that where I am, there ye may be also. (John 14:2-3)*

The Apostle Paul describes this return of Christ in detail:

> *But I would not have you to be ignorant, brethren, concerning them which are asleep, that ye sorrow not, even as others which have no hope. For if we believe that Jesus died and rose again, even so them also which sleep in Jesus will God bring with him. For this we say unto you by the word of the Lord, that we which are alive and remain unto the coming of the Lord shall not prevent them which are asleep. For the Lord himself shall descend from heaven with a shout, with the voice of the archangel, and with the trump of God: and the dead in Christ shall rise first: Then we which are alive and remain shall be caught up together with them in the clouds, to meet the Lord in*

the air: and so shall we ever be with the Lord.
Wherefore comfort one another with these words.
(1 Thessalonians 4:13-18)

This passage indicates that Christ Himself will return; there will be a resurrection of those who were believers when they died; there will be a catching up--a rapture--of living believers from earth to meet Christ in the air; and there will be a reunion between believers who have previously died, believers living at the time of the rapture, and the Lord Jesus Christ. The Bible teaches that no one knows the exact hour of the rapture, but that we can tell when it is near by observing the prophetic signs listed in Matthew 24.

Someday, you will either leave this world through the rapture or through death. If you die before the Lord's return and you are a believer, you will go immediately into the presence of the Lord:

> *We are confident, I say, and willing rather to be*
> *absent from the body, and to be present with the Lord.*
> *Wherefore we labour, that, whether present or absent,*
> *we may be accepted of him. For we must all appear*
> *before the judgment seat of Christ; that every one may*
> *receive the things done in his body, according to that*
> *he hath done, whether it be good or bad.*
> *(2 Corinthians 5:8-10)*

At the time of the final resurrection *"...all that are in the graves shall hear his voice, And shall come forth; they that have done good, unto the resurrection of life; and they that have done evil, unto the resurrection of damnation"* *(John 5:28-29).*

After a terrible time of great tribulation here on earth, there will be a final battle waged by God against the enemy forces of the Antichrist. At the conclusion of that time on earth, final judgment will occur. This is not something the believer needs to fear, however, because Psalm 91 guarantees that only with our eyes will we behold the judgment of the wicked.

The meaning of the word "judgment" includes holding a person accountable, examining evidence, determining guilt or innocence, and deciding penalties. God's ultimate desire is not to impose judgment, but that all men come to the knowledge of Jesus Christ:

> *For God sent not His Son into the world to condemn the world; but that the world through Him might be saved. (John 3:17)*

God does not want anyone to perish in sin:

> *The Lord is not slack concerning His promise, as some men count slackness; but is longsuffering to us-ward, not willing that any should perish, but that all should come to repentance. (2 Peter 3:9)*

Every person who has lived will someday experience judgment:

> *And the times of this ignorance God winked at; but now commandeth all men every where to repent; Because He hath appointed a day, in the which He will judge the world in righteousness...*
> *(Acts 17:30-31)*

Jesus said there will be two divisions of people at the time of final judgment: Believers and unbelievers:

Marvel not at this: for the hour is coming, in the which all that are in the graves shall hear his voice, And shall come forth; they that have done good, unto the resurrection of life; and they that have done evil, unto the resurrection of damnation. (John 5:28-29)

The Bible warns that, *"...every one of us shall give account of himself to God" (Romans 14:12)*. The Bible also declares that...

...we must all appear before the judgment seat of Christ; that every man may receive the things done in his body, according to that he hath done, whether it be good or bad. (2 Corinthians 5:10)

Believers need not fear because they will stand before God in the imputed righteousness of Jesus Christ. The judgment of true believers is not one of condemnation because a true believer cannot be condemned to eternal punishment. Through accepting Christ, he has already passed from spiritual death to eternal life:

Verily, verily, I say unto you, He that heareth my word, and believeth on Him that sent me, hath everlasting life, and shall not come into condemnation, but is passed from death unto life. (John 5:24)

Wicked unbelievers, however, will be judged and punished for their sin. Judgment of unbelievers is necessary because of their:

Sin against God's law: *For all have sinned, and come short of the glory of God...(Romans 3:23)*

Ungodliness: *But the heavens and the earth, which are now, by the same word are kept in store, reserved unto fire against the day of judgment and perdition of ungodly men. (2 Peter 3:7)*

Unrighteousness: *The Lord knoweth how to deliver the godly out of temptations, and to reserve the unjust unto the day of judgment to be punished. (2 Peter 2:9)*

Unbelief: *He that believeth on Him is not condemned; but he that believeth not is condemned already, because he hath not believed in the name of the only begotten Son of God. (John 3:18)*

Trespasses: *By the offence [trespass] of one, judgment came upon all men to condemnation... (Romans 5:18, AMP)*

Evil deeds: *And this is the condemnation, that light is come into the world, and men loved darkness rather than light, because their deeds were evil. (John 3:19)*

God will judge the wicked upon the basis of His Word. Jesus said:

> *And if any man hear my words and believe not, I judge him not: for I came not to judge the world, but to save the world. He that rejecteth me, and receiveth not my words, hath one that judgeth him: the word that I have spoken, the same shall judge him in the last day. (John 12:47-48)*

The assurance that true believers have regarding final judgment is that...

> *He who believes in Him [who clings to, trusts in, relies on Him] is not judged [he who trusts in Him*

never comes up for judgment; for him there is no rejection, no condemnation--he incurs no damnation]; but he who does not believe (cleave to, rely on, trust in Him) is judged already [he has already been convicted and has already received his sentence] because he has not believed in and trusted in the name of the only begotten Son of God. [He is condemned for refusing to let his trust rest in Christ's name.] The [basis of the] judgment (indictment, the test by which men are judged, the ground for the sentence) lies in this: the Light has come into the world, and people have loved the darkness rather than and more than the Light, for their works (deeds) were evil. For every wrongdoer hates (loathes, detests) the Light, and will not come out into the Light but shrinks from it, lest his works (his deeds, his activities, his conduct) be exposed and reproved. But he who practices truth [who does what is right] comes out into the Light; so that his works may be plainly shown to be what they are--wrought with God [divinely prompted, done with God's help, in dependence upon Him]. (John 3:18-21, AMP)

Our works--how we used the talents and abilities given to us by God--will be reviewed, but we will not experience the divine wrath of God's judgment for sin because Jesus bore the penalties for our sins.

The judgment of the wicked will result in a great separation:

The Son of Man will send forth His angels, and they will gather out of His kingdom all causes of offense [persons by whom others are drawn into error or sin] and all who do iniquity and act wickedly, And will cast them into the furnace of fire; there will be weeping and wailing and grinding of teeth. Then will

141

the righteous (those who are upright and in right standing with God) shine forth like the sun in the kingdom of their Father. Let him who has ears [to hear] be listening, and let him consider and perceive and understand by hearing. So shall it be at the end of the world: the angels shall come forth, and sever the wicked from among the just, And shall cast them into the furnace of fire: there shall be wailing and gnashing of teeth. (Matthew 13:41-43, 49-50, AMP)

On that great judgment day, the decision you have made regarding Jesus Christ will determine your destiny. That is why the Bible warns:

...Today if ye will hear his voice, harden not your hearts, as in the provocation...But with whom was he grieved forty years? Was it not with them that had sinned, whose carcases fell in the wilderness? And to whom sware he that they should not enter into his rest, but to them that believed not? So we see that they could not enter in because of unbelief.
(Hebrews 3:15-19)

After death, there is a great gulf between the saved and the lost (Luke 16:26). You must choose today who you will serve (Joshua 24:15). Your eternal destiny is determined by what you decide regarding Jesus Christ. Don't delay. If you aren't ready for judgment day, get ready. Right now. Today.

A Cause To Rejoice

It seems sad when we consider the judgment of the wicked that is to come, but the Bible indicates that we should actually rejoice when God judges sin. David declared:

Make a joyful noise unto the Lord, all the earth: make a loud noise, and rejoice, and sing praise. Sing unto the Lord with the harp; with the harp, and the voice of a psalm. With trumpets and sound of cornet make a joyful noise before the Lord, the King. Let the sea roar, and the fulness thereof; the world, and they that dwell therein. Let the floods clap their hands: let the hills be joyful together before the Lord; for he cometh to judge the earth: with righteousness shall he judge the world, and the people with equity.
(Psalm 98:4-9)

In this passage David says to make a joyful noise to the Lord. He says to rejoice loudly, sing praises, and praise God on the harp, the trumpets, and the cornet. Then David exhorts all of nature to rejoice. The reason? Because God is coming to judge the world with righteousness.

You will either be a witness to or a recipient of the judgment of the wicked based on your decision regarding Jesus Christ. So...

Let us hear the conclusion of the whole matter: Fear God, and keep his commandments: for this is the whole duty of man. For God shall bring every work into judgment, with every secret thing, whether it be good, or whether it be evil. (Ecclesiastes 12:13-14)

Chapter Eleven
Dealing With Disasters

"Because you have made the Lord,
who is my refuge, even the Most High,
your dwelling place,
No evil shall befall you,
nor shall any plague
come near your dwelling..."

From the beginning of this study of Psalm 91, the requirements for claiming its promises have been emphasized, the necessity of dwelling in the secret place and abiding under the shadow of the Almighty.

With verse nine of this beautiful manifest, these requirements are emphasized once again when the psalmist declares, *"Because you have made the Lord, who is my refuge, even the Most High, your dwelling place, no evil shall befall you, Nor shall any plague come near your dwelling..."*

The New American Standard renders "dwelling place" as *"your tent".* God's Word translation says because *"You have made the Most High your home, no harm will come to you."*

The Message Bible declares, *"Yes, because God's your refuge, the High God your very own home, evil can't get close to you, harm can't get through the door."*

The promises that follow in the remainder of Psalm 91 are dependent upon making the Lord your dwelling place. It is *because* you have made Him your refuge and dwelling place that no evil shall befall you, nor shall plagues come near your spiritual dwelling.

In verse one, we examined in detail what it means to dwell with the Lord in the secret place and learned that the name, "the Most High God" means "the possessor of heaven and earth".

In verse two, we discussed the meaning of a refuge, learning that God is our refuge--our place of security in times of trouble. If we abide in the secret place we are assured that *"...the eternal God is thy refuge, and underneath are the everlasting arms"... (Deuteronomy 33:27).*

In verses nine and ten, the psalmist assumes that the reader has made the Most High God their refuge and dwelling place. To those who have done this, he declares, *"No evil shall befall you, nor shall any plague come near your dwelling."* The Good News Bible says *"no disaster will strike you, no violence will come near your home".* The New Century Version states that *"Nothing bad will happen to you; no disaster will come to your home."* The New Living Translation states that *"no evil will conquer you".*

As you examine verses nine and ten in detail, you will need an understanding of what is meant by evil and plagues, and--most importantly--what it means when it promises that these things shall not come near your dwelling place.

Evil

Evil is any act of rebellion against God or contrary to His Word. It is wickedness that causes misunderstandings, pain, sorrow, alienation, and--in some cases--physical injury and death. Evil is any form of sin, transgression, rebellion, and disobedience. When you dwell in the secret place and abide in God's shadow, there are two categories of evil that cannot befall you. We are calling them personal evil and imposed evil.

Personal evil. If you want to maintain your intimate fellowship with God, you cannot live habitually in sin and continue to deliberately disobey God's Word:

> *No one who abides in Him [who lives and remains in communion with and in obedience to Him-- deliberately, knowingly, and habitually] commits (practices) sin. No one who [habitually] sins has either seen or known Him [recognized, perceived, or understood Him, or has had an experiential acquaintance with Him]. (1 John 3:6, AMP)*

You cannot continue to abide in the secret place of intimacy with God when you are habitually and purposefully sinning against Him:

> *Whosoever committeth sin transgresseth also the law: for sin is the transgression of the law. And ye know that he was manifested to take away our sins; and in him is no sin. Whosoever abideth in him sinneth not: whosoever sinneth hath not seen him, neither known him. Little children, let no man deceive you: he that doeth righteousness is righteous, even as he is righteous. He that committeth sin is of the devil; for the devil sinneth from the beginning. For this purpose the Son of God was manifested, that he might destroy the works of the devil. Whosoever is born of God doth not commit sin; for his seed remaineth in him: and he cannot sin, because he is born of God. (1 John 3:4-9)*

This does not mean that every time you sin you fall out of relationship with God, nor does it mean that as a believer you will never again commit a sin. This passage concerns continually and willfully living in known sin.

147

A good analogy is the relationship between a husband and wife. When they have a misunderstanding or one wrongs the other, it affects their fellowship. Their communication and intimacy are affected until the matter is settled and the wrong is made right. Their relationship as husband and wife is not severed, but their fellowship is affected.

The same is true of your relationship with God. You don't lose your salvation and need to get born-again every time you sin. You are still a Christian, but your intimate fellowship in the secret place is affected until you repent of your sin:

> *If we say that we have no sin , we deceive ourselves, and the truth is not in us. If we confess our sins, he is faithful and just to forgive us our sins, and to cleanse us from all unrighteousness. (1 John 1:8-9)*

Jesus made the request for forgiveness part of the prayer which He taught His followers to pray daily. He did this so that their fellowship with God could be renewed each day because no evil can dwell in God's presence (Psalm 5:4).

In the example of a married couple, if things are not made right between them and they continue to wrong each other, eventually not only is their fellowship affected, their relationship is damaged. Broken fellowship that remains unresolved may result in separation or divorce--a shattered relationship. Living in known sin, rejecting God's Word and failing to repent, may ultimately affect your relationship with God as well. God, the one who hates divorce, divorced Israel because of their continuous, unrepentant evil (Jeremiah 3:8). Not until they repented was the relationship restored.

Repeatedly in scripture we are told to depart from evil which is described as transgression, disobedience, lawlessness, iniquity, missing the mark, and trespasses. You must guard against personal evil that would invade the sanctity of your secret place and get you off course from walking in God's shadow. God said He will protect you from evil when you live in the secret place, but if you deliberately choose to walk in your own sinful ways, the promise of protection is void.

Imposed evil. Personal evil is one aspect of evil. "Imposed evil" is the term we are using to describe the second type of evil from which God protects you in the secret place. This is not the evil resulting from your own sin, rather it is evil brought against you by the enemy, his demonic forces, and those who yield themselves to such wicked powers.

As we learned in Psalm 91:4, God has provided spiritual weapons that protect you, equip you to combat evil powers, and enable you to be victorious over the enemy (Ephesians 6:10-18). The Bible promises:

> *No weapon that is formed against thee shall prosper; and every tongue that shall rise against thee in judgment thou shalt condemn. This is the heritage of the servants of the Lord, and their righteousness is of me, saith the Lord. (Isaiah 54:17)*

Nothing that rises up against you can gain access to your secret place with God. The promise doesn't say weapons won't be formed against you or that people won't say bad things about you. It promises that these attacks will not be effective because you are secure in your secret place. Even if a believer is killed by someone wielding a weapon, the evil has not truly prospered because he is already living eternal life. He will just continue to live it on the other side of the grave if he dies. So in reality, there is no way that any carnal weapon can affect you permanently if you dwell in the secret place with God.

Plagues

To those who make the Lord their refuge and remain in the secret place, God not only promises protection from evil but also from plagues. The word "plague", as used in the Bible, most often refers to judgment in the form of a calamity or sickness caused by sin.

The first recorded use of the word "plague" in the Bible is in Exodus 11:1 where God declared that He would bring one last plague upon Pharaoh and Egypt because of their refusal to set His people free. The phrase "I will bring one more plague" confirms that the previous judgments--water turned to blood, frogs, gnats or lice, flies, diseased livestock, boils, thunder and hail, locust, and darkness--were also plagues sent from God. The plagues of Egypt were not just the display of the meaningless wrath of some angry god. The Lord's declaration regarding the calamities was that *"... ye shall know that I am the Lord your God."* God wanted the Egyptians to recognize that He was God. Each plague was actually an opportunity for repenting and acknowledging Him as the true God.

The last plague was the death of the first-born son in every Egyptian home. The people of Israel, however, were given specific instructions regarding applying the blood of a slain lamb to their dwellings to assure their protection from this judgment:

> *And the blood shall be to you for a token upon the houses where ye are: and when I see the blood, I will pass over you, and the plague shall not be upon you to destroy you, when I smite the land of Egypt. (Exodus 12:13)*

As a believer, secure in your secret place and following carefully in God's shadow, you need not fear His judgment. The blood of Jesus--God's perfect lamb--is upon your life, and no plague of His judgment will come near you. You will experience no divine displeasure when you continue to dwell in the secret place.

Throughout scripture, the word "plague" continues to be associated with judgment that comes upon those who are not walking God's way. In Numbers chapters 11-12, judgment came upon God's people because of their sinful complaining spirits--a good warning to us all. In Numbers 14, a plague came upon the spies who returned from the promised land with a negative report:

> *And the men, which Moses sent to search the land, who returned, and made all the congregation to murmur against him, by bringing up a slander upon the land, Even those men that did bring up the evil report upon the land, died by the plague before the Lord. But Joshua the son of Nun, and Caleb the son of Jephunneh, which were of the men that went to search the land, lived still. (Numbers 14:36-38)*

When you studied Psalm 91:2, you learned the power of confession. Death and life are in the power of your tongue. Be careful about receiving and giving negative reports so you will not experience calamities brought on by your own words.

In Numbers 16, a plague resulted from the rebellion of Korah against the leadership God had set in place--another great warning to believers.

Plagues as judgment from God continue right up through the end-time. Revelation 16:21 prophesies that men will refuse to repent and will blaspheme God because of the plagues that come upon them during the tribulation.

Remember: As a true believer abiding in the secret place, you will not be cursed with a plague resulting from God's judgment:

> *And it shall come to pass, if thou shalt hearken diligently unto the voice of the Lord thy God, to observe and to do all his commandments which I command thee this day, that the Lord thy God will set thee on high above all nations of the earth: And all these blessings shall come on thee, and overtake thee, if thou shalt hearken unto the voice of the Lord thy God. (Deuteronomy 28:1-2)*

A long list of blessings that you will experience as an obedient believer follow this passage. Deuteronomy 28:58-61 reveals just the opposite: A long list of judgments resulting from not walking in obedience to the Word of God.

The Lord promised that He would not send judgments upon those who obey God's Word. As a believer, if you experience something that medical science calls a plague don't think you are under judgment from God because plagues also result from germs and disease, not just because of personal sin.

Sickness and disease exist in this sinful, fallen world, and just because someone is afflicted with something that might be called a plague does not mean they are under God's judgment. As a believer, you are not immune to such attacks, but healing for sickness and disease is provided through the atonement of Jesus Christ. In the New Testament, the woman with the issue of blood was healed of a plague when she touched the hem of Christ's garment (Matthew 9:20-22).

Your Dwelling Place

Just because someone is affected by evil or a plague does not mean they are under God's judgment, nor does it mean they have abandoned their secret place of intimate fellowship with God. In chapter eighteen of this study, you will learn about Job, a righteous man who lost his home, his family, his income, and his health--not because of sin, but because of an attack of Satan (Job chapters 1-2).

Despite these terrible attacks, Job's true dwelling place was not affected. Your physical house might collapse in a hurricane or tornado just like the house of the sinner living next door to you. Your physical house is gone, but it does not affect your true dwelling place. You have lost a house, but not your true home.

Let's read the promise again:

> *Because thou hast made the Lord, which is my refuge, even the most High, thy habitation; There shall no evil befall thee, neither shall any plague come nigh thy dwelling. (Psalm 91:9-10)*

And where is your true dwelling? It is not your house that is made of wood, plaster, or stones. You learned in Psalm 91:1 that your true dwelling is the secret place of intimate fellowship with the Lord. Job lost his house, but he didn't lose his dwelling place in God, for despite all of these calamities...

> *Then Job arose, and rent his mantle, and shaved his head, and fell down upon the ground, and worshipped, And said, Naked came I out of my mother's womb, and naked shall I return thither: the Lord gave, and the Lord hath taken away; blessed be*

the name of the Lord. In all this Job sinned not, nor charged God foolishly. (Job 1:20-22)

How could Job worship at a time like that? Because although his material house was gone, he had not lost his real dwelling. Throughout his trial, despite his questions and laments, Job never abandoned his secret place.

Psalm 91:9-10 reveals that as long as the real you--your spiritual man--remains in intimate fellowship with God, your true spiritual dwelling is not affected. Even if your material house collapses or the physical house of your body is afflicted as Job's was, your true dwelling remains secure.

Hebrews 10:34-35 describes the godly attitude toward possessions that was held by the first believers, recalling *"For ye...took joyfully the spoiling of your goods, knowing in yourselves that ye have in heaven a better and an enduring substance. Cast not away therefore your confidence, which hath great recompense of reward."* These believers were not robbed of their joy when their material possessions were lost because they knew they had a more enduring substance in heaven that could not be affected by calamity.

The hall of faith in Hebrews 11 speaks of those who...

> *...through faith subdued kingdoms, wrought righteousness, obtained promises, stopped the mouths of lions, Quenched the violence of fire, escaped the edge of the sword, out of weakness were made strong, waxed valiant in fight, turned to flight the armies of the aliens. Women received their dead raised to life again: and others were tortured, not accepting deliverance; that they might obtain a better resurrection. (Hebrews 11:33-35)*

But this chapter also speaks of those who were destitute, afflicted, tormented, and martyred as being men and women of faith. Some were delivered, some were not. Peter was supernaturally delivered from prison, but John the Baptist died in prison. God did not love Peter more than John. Everything that happens isn't about you, but it is about God's purpose and plans. John's mission in life was accomplished. Peter's was just starting.

God will reveal some answers regarding calamities that affect you, but others He may choose not to reveal because:

> *The secret things belong unto the Lord our God: but those things which are revealed belong unto us and to our children for ever, (Deuteronomy 29:29)*

You must come to the realization that there will be some things you will not understand, some circumstances for which there is no good explanation. Like Job, you may not receive the answer to your difficult questions but what you can be assured of is that:

> *...all things work together for good to them that love God, to them who are the called according to his purpose. (Romans 8:28)*

If you believe this promise that as a believer who is called according to God's purpose all things are working for your good--even things that appear to be evil--then you will never be tempted to abandon your secret place. Evil will not come near your real dwelling place of intimacy in the shadow of Almighty God.

When Jesus revealed details of His forthcoming death, the scriptures record that many of His disciples turned back from following Him:

From that time many of his disciples went back, and walked no more with him. Then said Jesus unto the twelve, Will ye also go away? Then Simon Peter answered him, Lord, to whom shall we go? Thou hast the words of eternal life. And we believe and are sure that thou art that Christ, the Son of the living God. (John 6:66-69)

When difficult times come, will you turn away from God or will you remain secure in your secret place? When you face a calamity you don't understand, do not abandon your relationship with God. Evil and plagues will either drive you to the Lord or away from Him.

Let go of your anger, pain, bitterness, and unanswered questions. Like Job, you may have lost your house, your family, your possessions, and your business. Your mate may have turned against you. But your real dwelling place --your refuge of security and safety--is still there!

Come on back to the secret place.

SECTION FOUR
DIVINE PARTNERS

*"For He shall give His angels charge over you, to
keep you in all your ways.
They shall bear you up in their hands, lest you
dash your foot against a stone.
You shall tread upon the lion
and the cobra,
The young lion and the serpent
you shall trample underfoot."*

(Psalm 91:11-13)

Chapter Twelve
Activating The Angels

"For He shall give His angels charge over you,
to keep you in all your ways.
They shall bear you up in their hands,
lest you dash your foot against a stone."

In 2 Kings chapter 6, the biblical record shows the enemy nation of Syria surrounding a small town called Dothan where the Prophet Elisha was staying. When Elisha's servant, Gehazi, saw the great enemy host poised to attack he became fearful:

> *And when the servant of the man of God was risen early, and gone forth, behold, an host compassed the city both with horses and chariots. And his servant said unto him, Alas, my master! how shall we do? (2 Kings 6:15)*

The Prophet Elisha answered Gehazi and said:

> *...Fear not: for they that be with us are more than they that be with them. And Elisha prayed, and said, Lord, I pray thee, open his eyes, that he may see. And the Lord opened the eyes of the young man; and he saw: and, behold, the mountain was full of horses and chariots of fire round about Elisha. (2 Kings 6:16-17)*

Elisha prayed that Gehazi would be able to see the angelic hosts surrounding and protecting them. God answered his prayer, opened Gehazi's eyes, and allowed him to actually see the invisible angelic host.

Some believers have been privileged to see angels, as did Gehazi and Elisha. You may have never seen an angel and perhaps you never will in this life, but that is not as important as understanding their ministry and how angels are activated in your behalf.

Psalm 91 teaches that as a believer, you are surrounded by an angelic heavenly host. Those who dwell in the secret place and live under the shadow of God are promised, *"He shall give His angels charge over you, to keep you in all your ways. They shall bear you up in their hands, lest you dash your foot against a stone" (Psalm 91:11).*

The Amplified Version states, *"For He will give His angels [especial] charge over you to accompany and defend and preserve you in all your ways [of obedience and service]. They shall bear you up on their hands, lest you dash your foot against a stone."*

The English Standard Version says angels will *"guard you in all your ways"*. The Holman Bible states *"He will give His angels orders concerning you"*. The New International Readers Version says that *"The Lord will command his angels to take good care of you. They will lift you up in their hands. Then you won't trip over a stone."*

The Message Bible says *"If you stumble, they'll catch you; their job is to keep you from falling."* The Wycliff Bible interprets this passage: *"For God hath commanded to his angels of thee; that they keep thee in all thy ways. (For God hath commanded his angels to be all around thee; so that they keep thee safe on all thy ways.) They shall bear thee in the hands; lest peradventure thou hurt thy foot at a stone. (They shall lift thee up with their hands; lest thou hurt thy foot on a stone.)"*

About Angels

The word "He" in Psalm 91:11 means God, so the first thing we learn about angels in this passage is that they are under God's command. The Bible also teaches that angels--as everything else in the universe--were created by God:

> *All things were made by Him; and without Him was not any thing made that was made. (John 1:3)*

> *For by Him were all things created, that are in Heaven, and that are in earth, visible and invisible, whether they be thrones, or dominions, or principalities, or powers; all things were created by Him and for Him. (Colossians 1:16)*

Satan was originally created as a heavenly angel. His name, Lucifer, meant "light bearer" (Isaiah 14:12). Lucifer was decked with precious stones set in gold and he apparently led worship on God's holy mountain (Ezekiel 28:13). Through pride, Satan sinned against God, was required to depart from Heaven, and took some rebellious angels with him (Ezekiel 28:12-17). Satan and these fallen angels are evil forces that are operative in the world today:

> *And no marvel; for Satan himself is transformed into an angel of light. Therefore it is no great thing if his ministers also be transformed as the ministers of righteousness; whose end shall be according to their works. (2 Corinthians 11:14-15)*

Satanic forces are quite deceptive and can even appear as beautiful beings of light. This is why you need to be sure that reports from people who claim to have seen angels line up with what is taught in the written Word of God.

The angels mentioned in Psalm 91:11 are the ones who remained true to God. These are the ones who are given charge over believers. The word "charge" in Psalm 91:11 means to accompany, defend, and preserve. Angels are under God's control, are dispatched at His Word, and are sent to minister in behalf of true believers.

Erroneously, some people believe their departed loved ones become angels. There is no scriptural support for this. Others are obsessed with angels, praying to them or worshipping them. This is forbidden in scripture. There are some believers who totally ignore the ministry of angels because they do not understand their function, while others base their understanding only on reports of people who claim to have seen an angel.

As in every area of doctrine, you must base your beliefs on God's Word. A study of all the Bible teaches about angels is beyond the scope of this chapter, but here are some basic scriptural facts about them:

-They are created beings: Colossians 1:16.
-They sometimes function in human form, i.e. they talk, eat, etc: Psalms 78:25.
-They are active in the affairs of men: Genesis 19:1,15; Hebrews 1:14.
-They are not to be worshipped: Colossians 2:18.
-They sometimes function in companies: Psalms 68:17; Matthew 26:53.
-Angels are innumerable: Hebrews 12:22.
-They wear white garments: John 20:12.
-There are different kinds of angels, good and evil: Ezekiel 10:5; Jude 9.
-There are different ranks of angels: Ephesians 6:12; Revelation 12:7.
-They do not marry: Matthew 22:30.

-Michael and Gabriel are the only angels mentioned by
  name: Revelation 12:7-10; Daniel 8:15-17, 9:21-24.
-They are assigned by God to minister and relay messages
  to believers: Hebrews 1:14.
-You are sometimes unaware that angels are ministering in
  your behalf: Hebrews 13:2.
-Angels are dispatched by the Word of God: Psalm 103:20.
-They minister to physical needs: 1 Kings19:5-6.
-They deliver believers from judgment: Genesis 19:15.
-They protect believers from danger: Psalm 34:6-7.
-They assist God in answering prayer: Daniel 9:23.
-They demonstrate how to worship: Psalm 148:2.
-They escort you in death: Luke 16:22;
-They strengthen you: Luke 22:43.
-They watch over you: Daniel 10:17-18;
  1 Corinthians 4:9, Ephesians 3:10; Hebrews 12:1.
-They rejoice when sinners repent: Luke 15:10.
-They execute warfare on your behalf: Exodus 33:2.
-They are active in evangelism: Acts 10:1-3,5; 8:26.
-They are active in the affairs of nations: Daniel 10:12-13.
-They can be visible or invisible: Numbers 22:22;
  Hebrews 13:2.
-They need no rest: Revelation 4:8.
-They can descend and ascend to heaven: Genesis 28:12;
  John 1:51.
-They are sometimes involved in controlling nature:
  Revelation 7:1.

Angels were active throughout the Old Testament, including
at the destruction of Sodom (Genesis 19:1); announcing the
birth of Isaac to Abraham and Sarah (Genesis 18:10-14);
ministering to Hagar (Genesis 21:17-18); appearing to Jacob
(Genesis 28:12, 31:11, 32:1, 48:16), Moses (Exodus 3:2),
Balaam (Numbers 22:22-23), Joshua (Joshua 5:13-15),
Gideon (Judges 6:11-40), Manoah (Judges 13:15-18), Samson
(Judges 13), Elijah (1 Kings 19:5-8), Elisha (2 Kings 6:14-

17), Daniel (Daniel 6:22), and Zechariah (Zechariah 1:14-16). They also destroyed an entire Assyrian army (2 Kings 19:35), and Isaiah 37:36 records that one angel defeated 185,000 men!

Angels were involved in the events in the life, death, and resurrection of Jesus. They predicted His birth to Mary (Luke 1:26-37) and Joseph (Matthew 1:20-21). They announced His name (Matthew 1:21) and directed His family's flight to Egypt to escape Herod (Matthew 2:13,20). They ministered to Jesus after His temptation (Matthew 4:11) and at Gethsemane (Luke 22:43), they rolled away the stone at the garden tomb (Matthew 28:2), announced His resurrection (Matthew 28:5-7), and were present when He appeared to Mary of Magdala (John 20:11-14). They were present when He ascended back into Heaven (Acts 1:10-11) and they will be present when He returns to earth again (Matthew 16:27).

Angels were active in the early church. They rescued Peter from prison (Acts 12:7-9), struck Herod dead for blasphemy (Acts 12:23), directed Cornelius (Acts 10:3), and were with Paul during his fateful ocean voyage (Acts 27:22-25).

Angels will be instrumental in events at the return of Jesus. A great number of them will appear with Him in the clouds (2 Thessalonians 1:7). Angels will be like reapers (Matthew 13:39), separating the righteous from the wicked (Matthew 13:41,49) and they will carry out many of the end-time events recorded in the book of Revelation (Revelation chapters 1-3, 5, 7-11, 14, and 16-22).

In All Your Ways

One of the keys to understanding Psalm 91:11 is found in the phrase *"...in all your ways" (Psalm 91:11)*. Remember at the beginning of this Psalm in verse one you learned that the promises in this chapter are for those who abide in the shadow of the Almighty. If you are in someone's shadow, it means you are walking the same way they are going.

Note that the promise in verse eleven is that angels will keep you in all your ways. If you are a true believer, your way is God's way. The Amplified Version translates this *"in all your ways of obedience and service".*

Don't expect the angels to take charge when you are out sinning in the devil's territory. The protection promised in this chapter is to those walking in the way of obedience and service, following in the shadow of the Almighty. God may graciously protect you when you are straying contrary to His way, but the promise is only guaranteed to those walking in God's shadow.

Did you realize that Satan knows this Psalm? He actually quoted a portion of Psalm 91 during the temptation of Jesus:

> *And he (Satan) brought him (Jesus) to Jerusalem, and set him on a pinnacle of the temple, and said unto him, If thou be the Son of God, cast thyself down from hence: For it is written, He shall give his angels charge over thee, to keep thee: And in their hands they shall bear thee up, lest at any time thou dash thy foot against a stone. (Luke 4:9-11)*

Actually, Satan misquoted this verse. Did you note what he omitted? He left out the phrase *"in all your ways".* In essence, He was saying, "Go ahead Jesus. Do your own thing. You can even do something foolish and prideful because you are kept by the angels." But Jesus knew better. He knew the promise of being kept by the angels was only to those walking in their designated way, which--when you walk with God--is His way.

165

If you say that you are abiding in the secret place, you should walk as Jesus walked because *"He that saith he abideth in him ought himself also so to walk, even as he walked" (1 John 2:6).* You should walk in newness of life (Romans 6:4) and in the Spirit, rather than in the flesh. Galatians 5 explains what this means and how to do it:

> *This I say then, Walk in the Spirit, and ye shall not fulfil the lust of the flesh. For the flesh lusteth against the Spirit, and the Spirit against the flesh: and these are contrary the one to the other: so that ye cannot do the things that ye would. But if ye be led of the Spirit, ye are not under the law. Now the works of the flesh are manifest, which are these; Adultery, fornication, uncleanness, lasciviousness, Idolatry, witchcraft, hatred, variance, emulations, wrath, strife, seditions, heresies, Envyings, murders, drunkenness, revellings, and such like: of the which I tell you before, as I have also told you in time past, that they which do such things shall not inherit the kingdom of God. But the fruit of the Spirit is love, joy, peace, longsuffering, gentleness, goodness, faith, Meekness, temperance: against such there is no law. And they that are Christ's have crucified the flesh with the affections and lusts. If we live in the Spirit, let us also walk in the Spirit. (Galatians 5:16-25)*

Angels are given charge over you as you walk God's way, remain in His shadow, and live your life in the Spirit rather than in the flesh.

Activating The Angels

Angels are not your personal errand boys and you cannot command them to do your selfish bidding. They are not entertainers, nor are they just spectators of what is going on in your life. Angels are divine messengers dispatched by the Word of God:

> *Bless the Lord, you His angels, who excel in strength, who do His word, Heeding the voice of His word. (Psalm 103:20)*

Angels heed the voice of God's Word. Negative words of fear and unbelief do nothing to improve your situation when you face challenges in life. Speak God's Word into your circumstances, and angels will be dispatched to minister in your behalf. As long as you are walking God's way and speaking His Word, the angels are active. Of course in order to do this, you must know God's Word and that knowledge only comes by applying yourself diligently to study it:

> *Study to shew thyself approved unto God, a workman that needeth not to be ashamed, rightly dividing the word of truth. (2 Timothy 2:15)*

As a believer, the angels of God encamp around you. The Bible says, *"The angel of the Lord encampeth round about them that fear him, and delivereth them" (Psalm 34:7).* If you fear God--meaning that you respect and honor Him--an angel camps out with you. (One is camping out right now here in this room as the words of this chapter are being written!)

From this brief overview of angels we see that they are active in the lives of believers to bring messages from God. They minister to believers to guide, provide, protect, deliver, strengthen, encourage, bring answers to prayer, and attend them at the time of death. As believers, we can respect angels, appreciate their ministries, activate them through speaking God's Word, and admire their example of worship, obedience, and allegiance to God.

Offending The Angels

Can you offend these supernatural beings of God and what happens if you do so? To answer this, let's examine the scriptures.

Negative words. Angels are activated by God's Word, so that means negative words of rebellion, fear, and unbelief hinder them from functioning. God dispatched an angel to go before Israel as they traveled through the wilderness:

> *Behold, I send an Angel before thee, to keep thee in the way, and to bring thee into the place which I have prepared. Beware of him, and obey his voice, provoke him not; for he will not pardon your transgressions: for my name is in him. But if thou shalt indeed obey his voice, and do all that I speak; then I will be an enemy unto thine enemies, and an adversary unto thine adversaries. (Exodus 23:20-22)*

God appointed an angel to keep His people in the way so they could safely arrive at their destination, but Israel's constant complaining resulted in judgment from God (Numbers chapters 11, 12, 14, and 24). Believing and confessing the negative reports about giants in the land and refusing to enter in and claim it resulted in the death of an entire generation (Numbers 13-14). Rebellious words also resulted in the deaths of Korah and his followers (Numbers 16) and a plague followed the false accusations recorded in Numbers 16:41-50.

So what happened to the angel who was dispatched to keep the Israelites in the way and bring them safely to the promised land? In these instances--all involving negative speaking--the ministry of the angel was hindered because the people were no longer walking God's way and confessing His Word. They provoked and offended their angel.

The Word declares that *"Death and life are in the power of the tongue: and they that love it shall eat the fruit thereof" (Proverbs 18:21).* Each day you will either speak words of death or life into the circumstances you face. Do not provoke the angels with negative words that hinder their ministry in your behalf.

Unbelief. In Luke 1:8-20, an angel appeared to Zacharias and announced the he would have a son. Because of his advanced age and the barrenness of his wife, Zacharias did not believe the angel and demanded a sign.

He got a sign all right! He was stricken mute until his son, John, was born (verse 20). Only when he began to speak in faith and confirm the name given by the angel for the baby was his tongue once again loosed.

Unbelief affects your testimony, just as Zacharias's speech was affected. If he had believed, as Mary did when the angel gave her news of Christ's birth, then Zacharias could have joyously proclaimed the message to his wife, family, and friends. Don't let unbelief hinder the ministry of angels in your life and render you mute spiritually.

Pride. In Acts 12:21-23, King Herod appeared before the people dressed in his regal garments and sitting on his beautiful throne. Awed by this display of power and wealth, the people began to call him a god and he did nothing to stop it. Immediately, an angel of the Lord struck him because he did not give glory to God. He was eaten by worms and died (verse 23). Angels can't tolerate pride because pride is one of the things God hates--most likely because it was the first sin and is the root of all sin (Proverbs 6:17). God resists the proud (James 4:6), so it is obvious that proud people will not be assisted by angels if God is resisting them.

Willful disobedience. Read the story of Balaam in Numbers 22. Balaam was a prophet who, in disobedience to God's command, went with messengers from Moab in response to the request of an evil king. On the way, an angel appeared in the roadway to stop him. The donkey Balaam was riding could see the angel, and stepped aside in fear. In so doing, the donkey crushed Balaam's foot against the wall and an angel spoke through the animal, rebuking Balaam for his disobedience. When you willfully disobey God, instead of ministering to you the angels will oppose you.

Unconfessed sin. Unconfessed sin prevents angels from working in your life. Read the story of the lame man at the pool of Bethesda in John 5:1-15. Although an angel frequently stirred the waters for healing, this man had lain there for 38 years and never made it into the pool. When Jesus asked him if he wanted to be healed, his answer was not a resounding "Yes!" Instead he said, "*Sir, I have no man, when the water is troubled, to put me into the pool: but while I am coming, another steppeth down before me" (John 5:7).* He was so busy complaining and feeling sorry for himself that he didn't realize who was standing right there before him. He was looking for a man to help him, rather than looking to God. After Jesus healed the lame man, He told him, "*... Behold, thou art made whole: sin no more, lest a worse thing come unto thee" (John 5:14).* Not all infirmity is caused by personal sin (John 9:3) but apparently this man's disability was related to his sin. For decades, his sinful, complaining spirit had prevented the work of angels in his life. The angels had come many times to minister over the years, but this man needed more than an angel could give. He needed forgiveness for sin.

Stones, Lions, And Serpents

Angels are given charge over you as you walk God's way and they will bear you up in their hands. Note that the term used in this passage is "angels", not just one guardian angel. Aren't you glad for that? Some of us need a host of them to help us face the tremendous challenges we experience in our lives and ministries!

Angels are given charge over you so that you will not dash your foot against a stone. A "stone" represents minor obstacles along the way that can impede your Christian walk and prevent you from reaching your divine destiny.

Have you ever noticed when you are hiking how a small stone can hinder your progress? You may have all the right hiking gear--your backpack is filled with proper supplies, food, water, a map, and a compass--but if you get a stone in your shoe you begin to limp along the way. At first, it will cause minor discomfort and slow you down. Eventually, it will stop you completely if you don't take time to eliminate it.

So it is with what we call "little sins." Song of Solomon 2:15 speaks of the "little foxes that spoil the vine." There are actually no little sins, because sin is sin in God's sight and little "stones" can impede your progress just as much as major obstacles. The Bible warns:

> *Ye did run well; who did hinder you that ye should not obey the truth? This persuasion cometh not of him that calleth you. A little leaven leaveneth the whole lump. (Galatians 5:7-9)*

Leaven as used in this verse represents evil and--like leaven-- evil spreads to penetrate the whole loaf. James warns against another "little" problem:

Even so the tongue is a little member, and boasteth great things. Behold, how great a matter a little fire kindleth! (James 3:5)

Angels can keep you from these and many other "stones" you encounter in the way--and they will do so as you continue to walk in God's shadow. Like David, you will be able to testify:

For thou hast delivered my soul from death, mine eyes from tears, and my feet from falling. I will walk before the Lord in the land of the living.
(Psalm 116:8-9)

When I said, My foot slippeth; thy mercy, O Lord, held me up. (Psalm 94:18)

Those who walk in the wisdom of God's Word are promised:

Then shalt thou walk in thy way safely, and thy foot shall not stumble. When thou liest down, thou shalt not be afraid: yea, thou shalt lie down, and thy sleep shall be sweet. Be not afraid of sudden fear, neither of the desolation of the wicked, when it cometh. For the Lord shall be thy confidence, and shall keep thy foot from being taken. (Proverbs 3:23-26)

Angels protect you from minor situations, represented in this verse by stones. They also protect you from major threats represented in Psalm 91:13 by lions and serpents:

For he shall give his angels charge over thee, to keep thee in all thy ways. They shall bear thee up in their hands, lest thou dash thy foot against a stone. Thou

shalt tread upon the lion and adder: the young lion
and the dragon shalt thou trample under feet.
(Psalm 91:11-13)

These major challenges--spiritual lions and serpents--are the subjects of the next two chapters.

Chapter Thirteen
Treading On Lions

"...You shall tread upon
the lion and the young lion..."

Do not think that the secret place is without challenges. Lions and serpents are close! Psalm 91:13 declares, *"You shall tread upon the lion and the cobra, The young lion and the serpent you shall trample underfoot" (verse 13, NKJ).*

This chapter explains the spiritual analogy of lions. The next chapter focuses on the analogy of snakes. This verse is not speaking of actual lions and snakes, but it is comparing the devil and his demonic forces to lions and snakes, using natural analogies to illustrate spiritual truths.

Lions represent visible problems, while snakes represent more concealed challenges. Some problems--like lions--are immediately recognizable. Others, like snakes that are concealed in rocks or grass, are not as easily seen but are equally as deadly. The good news is that although you are surrounded by lions and snakes, as long as you abide in the secret place you will be able to tread and trample upon them without harm.

The Good News Bible states you will trample down *"fierce lions"* and the New Century Version says *"strong lions"*. The New International Readers Version says you will *"crush mighty lions"*.

The Apostle Peter drew a spiritual analogy between the enemy, Satan, and lions when he wrote:

Be sober, be vigilant; because your adversary the devil, as a roaring lion, walketh about, seeking whom he may devour: Whom resist stedfast in the faith, knowing that the same afflictions are accomplished in your brethren that are in the world. (1 Peter 5:8-9)

Your adversary is not your mate, your kids, or your coworker. Your adversary is the devil and he is described as a roaring lion seeking someone to devour. The Bible uses many natural parallels to illustrate spiritual truths. For example, Jesus compared the spiritual needs of the world to a natural harvest field. He also drew spiritual analogies concerning the lilies of the field and the birds of the air to illustrate God's care for His people. In Psalm 91, the analogy of a lion is used to exemplify your spiritual enemy.

A roaring lion is dangerous because when it is roaring, it is trying to instill fear and seize territory. In the natural world, a lion's roar can be heard up to five miles away. In Psalm 91:13, a lion analogy is used to describe the spiritual enemy that is seeking to devour you. Satan is as a roaring lion, trying to instill fear and usurp your spiritual territory.

Peter indicates that Satan goes around seeking whom he may devour. The fact that Satan is seeking someone to devour means there are people he is unable to devour because they are alert to his attacks. This passage, penned by Peter under the inspiration of the Holy Spirit, will help you to recognize and deal effectively with this "roaring lion". It will enable you to be among those whom Satan cannot devour and--as Psalm 91:13 indicates--you will trample him underfoot.

Parallels Of Spiritual Truths

Here are some spiritual parallels drawn from the analogy of lions:

Lions are adversarial. If you meet a lion in the forest, he is your adversary! As a believer, you must recognize that Satan is your adversary and there is no neutral ground. He is out to get you!

Lions are nocturnal. They are active at night. Sinful places and sinful people as well as spiritual darkness are Satan's domain. As a child of light, you should not be hanging out with sinful people in places of darkness:

> *For once you were darkness, but now you are light in the Lord; walk as children of Light [lead the lives of those native-born to the Light]. For the fruit (the effect, the product) of the Light or the Spirit [consists] in every form of kindly goodness, uprightness of heart, and trueness of life. And try to learn [in your experience] what is pleasing to the Lord [let your lives be constant proofs of what is most acceptable to Him]. Take no part in and have no fellowship with the fruitless deeds and enterprises of darkness, but instead [let your lives be so in contrast as to] expose and reprove and convict them. For it is a shame even to speak of or mention the things that [such people] practice in secret. But when anything is exposed and reproved by the light, it is made visible and clear; and where everything is visible and clear there is light. Therefore He says, Awake, O sleeper, and arise from the dead, and Christ shall shine (make day dawn) upon you and give you light. Look carefully then how you walk! Live purposefully and worthily and accurately, not as the unwise and witless, but as wise (sensible, intelligent people).*
> *(Ephesians 5:8-17, AMP)*

Lions lie in wait for their prey. So does Satan. He is just waiting to prey on your weakness. He works through familiar spirits--spirits that are familiar with what strategies work on you. This is why you must always be alert to what is going on around you spiritually so you won't *"... give place to the devil" (Ephesians 4:27)*. Don't let Satan get his foot in the door!

Lions isolate their prey. On safaris into lion country, as long as you remain in the truck with the other tourists you are safe. If you step outside of the truck, you are isolated and become prey for the lions. Lions chase a herd of animals, then attack the weak or sick animal that separates from the herd. Spiritually, Satan wants to separate you from other believers through misunderstanding, strife, and confusion. Don't allow him to do this or you will become vulnerable to his attacks. The term "in Christ" is used repeatedly in the King James Version of the New Testament. You will be safe if you abide in Christ as part of a body of true believers. When you walk independently of Christ and the Church, you will eventually be devoured by the enemy.

Lions are territorial. Lions guard their territory and attack to gain new territory. When they are seeking to seize new territory or take over a pride of lions, they roar. A roaring lion is a dangerous lion. Satan is all about territory also. He wants to invade the territory of your marriage, your home, your emotions, your city, and your nation. Set a spiritual guard over your marriage, your children, your emotions, your ministry, etc. This will not make you immune to attacks, but it will prepare you to conquer your spiritual lion when he attacks. Jesus was prepared for Satan's attacks and met them with the Word of God. It is important that you don't spend time in the devil's territory--bars, drug houses, or places of the occult. Also, be especially alert when you are invading new spiritual territory for the advancement of the Gospel because you are challenging Satan's turf.

Lions are set on total destruction. Lions tear and devour their prey. When a lion takes control of a pride of lions, he kills all the cubs so that the young ones birthed will be of his bloodline. (Isn't it interesting that a group of lions is called a "pride" instead of a herd? And pride was Satan's sin!) Satan comes to kill, steal, and destroy you and your generations. Ezekiel 22:25 says that like a roaring lion, the enemy devours souls, treasures, and precious things. Satan wants to give birth to evil in your life through lust because "...*every man is tempted, when he is drawn away of his own lust, and enticed. Then when lust hath conceived, it bringeth forth sin: and sin, when it is finished, bringeth forth death" (James 1:14-15)*. The Amplified Version renders this as "*lust conceives and gives birth to sin*." Don't allow your generations to become Satan's prey. Don't let Satan kill and destroy your dreams. Don't let Satan give birth to the "cubs" of bitterness, hatred, unforgiveness, addictions, etc., in your life.

Lions attack if you turn and run. Do not retreat from your spiritual enemy or he will attack with a vengeance. Face the enemy in the power of the Lord. David faced a giant and did not retreat. A man named Benaiah killed two lion-like men and became known as a mighty man of God (2 Samuel 23:20-22 and 1 Chronicles 11:22). Gideon faced a massive army with only 300 soldiers and was victorious (Judges 7:7). These fearless men did not retreat. What could you do for God if you do not retreat? Fear is what causes retreat--which leads us to the next point.

Lions roar to instill fear in their prey. Faith energizes you to do great things for God. Fear paralyzes you. Paul declared, "*For God hath not given us the spirit of fear; but of power, and of love, and of a sound mind" (2 Timothy 1:7)*. As you learned in chapter eight of this study, fear is not of God, so rebuke it and reject it in the name of the Lord.

Lions give birth to lions. Psalm 91:13 refers to lions and to young lions. Lions conceive and give birth to lions. If you do not deal with the lions in your life--the addictions, wrong attitudes and emotions, and sins--then they will birth additional spiritual lions that will prey upon you. Joshua did not eliminate all of the giants in the land as God commanded. Had he done so, there never would have been a Goliath to rise up and challenge God's people. Goliath came from Gath where a "few giants" had been allowed to remain (Joshua 11:22). Giants give birth to giants. Lions give birth to lions. Unresolved lust conceives and births sin, which--when finished--results in death (James 1:15).

Four Major Strategies

Peter outlines four major strategies that will protect you from Satan's attacks:

> *Be well balanced (temperate, sober of mind), be vigilant and cautious at all times; for that enemy of yours, the devil, roams around like a lion roaring [in fierce hunger], seeking someone to seize upon and devour. Withstand him; be firm in faith [against his onset--rooted, established, strong, immovable, and determined], knowing that the same (identical) sufferings are appointed to your brotherhood (the whole body of Christians) throughout the world.*
> *(1 Peter 5:8-9, AMP)*

First, you must be self-controlled. Peter directs believers to be sober, which means to be in control. He says to be temperate, which means all things should be done in moderation. When you are bound by drugs, alcohol, anger, unforgiveness, etc., you are out of control. You are not sober spiritually when you allow these things to take control. You are no longer under the control of the Holy Spirit and you are in spiritual danger.

Second, you must be vigilant. Peter commands that you *"...be vigilant and cautious at all times"*. Vigilance means to be watchful and cautious. A tragic, but relevant example, is the 911 terrorist attack on America. Before this attack, Americans were not vigilant in many areas, especially in terms of airport security. After 911, the United States became more cautious because they finally realized there are enemies in the world whose aim is to destroy their nation. Be watchful and vigilant, because Satan wants to destroy you. Recognize that you live among spiritual lions that seek your destruction. You are not immune to their assaults any more than America is exempt from terrorist attacks.

Third, you must withstand Satan in the faith. Peter commands you to *"withstand him; be firm in faith [against his onset--rooted, established, strong, immovable, and determined]."* To do this, you must know the basics of your faith. The foundations of your faith are listed in Hebrews 6:1-3 and include repentance from dead works, faith toward God, the doctrine of baptisms, laying on of hands, resurrection of the dead, and eternal judgment.

Fourth, you must not isolate yourself. Don't spend time wondering "why me"? Peter says to realize that the same battles your are facing are being experienced by others. In the natural world, lions attack when an animal becomes isolated from the herd. The same is true in the spiritual world. Remain close to your Christian brothers and sisters and get connected with a local body of believers. They will help you ward off many attacks from spiritual lions because they have experienced similar challenges.

Lions Under Your Feet

In Psalm 91:13, the lions and young lions are depicted as being under your feet. Yes, you live among spiritual lions but you have power over them and all the power of the enemy: Jesus said, *"Behold, I give unto you power...over all the power of the enemy: and nothing shall by any means hurt you" (Luke 10:19).*

Satan is an imitator. Peter describes him *"**as** a roaring lion."* Did you know that Jesus is actually called the Lion of Judah? That is the name by which He is referred to in Revelation 5:5--and when our Lion roars, the seven thunders will utter their voices and God's plan will be fulfilled!

The only times in scripture that lions were successful in their attacks was when people were sinning by walking away from God. (For examples see Jeremiah 5:6 and 1 Kings 13:24.) To those who abide in the shadow of the Almighty, God promises, *"Thou shalt tread upon the lion and adder: the young lion and the dragon shalt thou trample under feet" (Psalm 91:13).*

Have you allowed spiritual lions to cause you to retreat? Have you been ignorant of Satan's strategies? Have you been fearful of his roars and isolated yourself from other believers? Have you been hanging out in places of darkness where spiritual lions congregate? The deception is over! You now know that Satan appears as a roaring lion and you have biblical strategies to combat him.

The Apostle Paul declared that he was delivered out of the mouth of the lion, You can have the same testimony (2 Timothy 4:17).

Before you turn to the next chapter, spend some time meditating on The Message translation of 1 Peter 5:8-9:

> *Keep a cool head. Stay alert. The Devil is poised to pounce, and would like nothing better than to catch you napping. Keep your guard up. You're not the only ones plunged into these hard times. It's the same with Christians all over the world. So keep a firm grip on the faith. The suffering won't last forever. It won't be long before this generous God who has great plans for us in Christ--eternal and glorious plans they are!--will have you put together and on your feet for good. He gets the last word; yes, he does.*

Chapter Fourteen
Trampling On Serpents

"...The cobra...and the serpent
you shall trample underfoot."

In the previous chapter, the spiritual analogy of lions was examined. This chapter remains focused on Psalm 91:13, as we analyze the spiritual analogy of snakes--identified in the New King James Version of the Bible as cobras and serpents.

The analogy of lions discussed in the previous chapter represents the easily recognizable threats, trials, and issues that you confront in life. Serpents, however, represent hidden dangers. They are concealed--like snakes hidden in grass or rocks--but are equally as deadly as lions. The cobra, named in this scripture, is one of the most deadly snakes in the natural world.

It is important to discern the meaning of this analogy. To do this, we must go back to the beginning of time in the Garden of Eden where the enemy first appeared in the form of a snake:

> *Now the serpent was more subtil than any beast of the field which the Lord God had made. And he said unto the woman, Yea, hath God said, Ye shall not eat of every tree of the garden? And the woman said unto the serpent, We may eat of the fruit of the trees of the garden: But of the fruit of the tree which is in the midst of the garden, God hath said, Ye shall not eat of it, neither shall ye touch it, lest ye die. And the serpent said unto the woman, Ye shall not surely die: For God doth know that in the day ye eat thereof, then your eyes shall be opened, and ye shall be as gods, knowing good*

and evil. And when the woman saw that the tree was good for food, and that it was pleasant to the eyes, and a tree to be desired to make one wise, she took of the fruit thereof, and did eat, and gave also unto her husband with her; and he did eat. And the eyes of them both were opened, and they knew that they were naked; and they sewed fig leaves together, and made themselves aprons. (Genesis 3:1-7)

Originally, the snake was one of the most sophisticated creatures created by God. It was more subtle--meaning more crafty and cunning--than any other creature. The serpent may have been able to actually talk, because Eve does not seem to find it strange to be conversing with him. This we do not know, but what we do know for sure is that Satan used the form of a serpent to lead mankind into sin and a curse was put upon the serpent because of this:

And the Lord God said unto the woman, What is this that thou hast done? And the woman said, The serpent beguiled me, and I did eat. And the Lord God said unto the serpent, Because thou hast done this, thou art cursed above all cattle, and above every beast of the field; upon thy belly shalt thou go, and dust shalt thou eat all the days of thy life: And I will put enmity between thee and the woman, and between thy seed and her seed; it shall bruise thy head, and thou shalt bruise his heel. (Genesis 3:13-15)

From this point on, snakes were used in scripture to represent evil. The Apostle Paul makes reference to this in 2 Corinthians 11:3 when he cautions, *"But I fear, lest by any means, as the serpent beguiled Eve through his subtilty, so your minds should be corrupted from the simplicity that is in Christ."* Satan is not stupid. He is crafty and cunning.

186

But Jesus promised, *"I give unto you power to tread on serpents and scorpions, and over all the power of the enemy: and nothing shall by any means hurt you" (Luke 10:19).*

We have power over all the power of the enemy. Do remember, however, the prerequisite of these Psalm 91 promises: You must dwell in the secret place and abide in the shadow of the Almighty. Don't think you can do your own thing and go your own way and not be an easy target for spiritual serpents.

Parallels Of Spiritual Truths

Using the natural example of snakes, there are numerous spiritual parallels that can be drawn to gain an understanding of the strategies of the enemy.

For example, the venom released by poisonous snakes when they attack affects your nerves, your blood, and your heart. Satan also attacks in these three areas. He attacks your nerve--your courage to live for God and fulfill your divine mandate. He attacks the work of the cross, trying to sabotage every benefit of Christ's blood in your life. He also targets your heart, trying to get you to focus your affections on things of the world.

Snakes in the natural world are difficult to see because they are disguised to look like the dirt, rocks, grass or trees in which they dwell. Likewise, Satan is also deceptive. He subtly blends right in and sets his traps for you. Something may look real good and if you are not walking in the shadow of the Almighty you may be deceived because Satan can appear as an angel of light (2 Corinthians 11:14). This is why many fall prey to false doctrines and cults.

187

The African tree viper freezes itself and sticks its neck out so that a passerby thinks it is simply a twig on a tree until it is too late to escape its deadly fangs. Satan is also an imitator. For example, God has a trinity and Satan has an unholy trinity. God has angels and Satan has fallen angels known as demons. God has a kingdom, and Satan has his kingdom. God has a plan for your life, and Satan has one too! It is up to you which plan you choose to follow.

In the natural world, there is a snake called a puff adder that can blow itself up and increase its size to make one think it is much bigger than it actually is. Satan uses this strategy also. When the Israeli spies went to view the promised land, ten of them returned with a negative report that there were giants in the land and that they felt like grasshoppers in their presence. Satan will always try to make problems, circumstances, and challenges appear bigger than they actually are. There will always be giants in the way of duty, but don't focus on them and don't develop a grasshopper mentality. The Apostle John declared, *"Ye are of God, little children, and have overcome them: because greater is he that is in you, than he that is in the world" (1 John 4:4).*

Some species of snakes in the natural world make frightening sounds by hissing or rattling. This is true in the spiritual world also. Satan will bring terrifying and anxious thoughts to mind in order to generate fear. Remember, as you learned in chapter eight of this study, God has not given you a spirit of fear, so if fear is not of God you know exactly where it is coming from (2 Timothy 1:7).

A snake captures its food in four different ways: Through a swift strike; by throwing its weight around its prey to overcome it; by holding the target in its fangs until the poison venom paralyzes it; and through constriction where it wraps itself around the victim and slowly squeezes out its life.

Do you see how these methods parallel those used by Satan in spiritual attacks? Sometimes Satan attacks with swift and deadly strikes. Other times he tries to squeeze the life out of you spiritually by the cares of the world and sinful weights and entanglements. Satan is always trying to "throw his weight around" to terrorize you and he especially wants to paralyze you with the deadly venom of bitterness, hatred, unforgiveness, and other negative emotions.

A snake locates its prey by picking up dust on its tongue which relays information to its brain. If you stand still, a snake cannot find you. Snakes locate you best when the dust is stirred up as you try to run away. Spiritually, you must also take a stand against the enemy and refuse to retreat:

> *Put on the whole armour of God, that ye may be able to stand against the wiles of the devil. For we wrestle not against flesh and blood, but against principalities, against powers, against the rulers of the darkness of this world, against spiritual wickedness in high places. Wherefore take unto you the whole armour of God, that ye may be able to withstand in the evil day, and having done all, to stand. Stand therefore, having your loins girt about with truth, and having on the breastplate of righteousness; And your feet shod with the preparation of the gospel of peace; Above all, taking the shield of faith, wherewith ye shall be able to quench all the fiery darts of the wicked. And take the helmet of salvation, and the sword of the Spirit, which is the word of God: Praying always with all prayer and supplication in the Spirit, and watching thereunto with all perseverance and supplication for all saints. (Ephesians 6:11-18)*

Avoiding Snakebite

Here are some ways to avoid snakebites in the natural world that are also applicable in the spiritual realm:

Learn to recognize poisonous snakes. Spiritually, you need to know your enemy, Satan, and learn to recognize his tactics.

Wear protective clothing. You need the spiritual armor listed in Ephesians 6:11-18.

Avoid known snake territory. Avoid environments of temptation and Satanic activity like bars, drug houses, and places where the occult is operative.

Walk with a friend. This illustrates the importance of being part of a local church and active as a member in the Body of Christ. Christian friends can help you through difficult times of Satanic attack.

Avoid walking in the dark. Snakes avoid direct sunlight and conceal themselves in the dark. As believers, we are no longer to walk as children of darkness but as children of light: *"This then is the message which we have heard of him, and declare unto you, that God is light, and in him is no darkness at all "* *(1 John 1:5).*

Do not run. In the natural world, snakes strike when they sense sudden movement. Spiritually, it is the same. Do not run from Satan. Resist him and he will flee from you!

Do not go out of your way to kill a snake. Thousands of people are bitten each year because they try to kill snakes without knowing anything about their habits or habitats. As believers, we are to resist the devil when he attacks and deliver those we encounter along the way who have been victimized by him, but we are not to deliberately seek him out. Jesus said:

> ...*Go ye into all the world, and preach the gospel to every creature. He that believeth and is baptized shall be saved; but he that believeth not shall be damned. And these signs shall follow them that believe; In my name shall they cast out devils; they shall speak with new tongues; They shall take up serpents; and if they drink any deadly thing, it shall not hurt them; they shall lay hands on the sick, and they shall recover. (Mark 16:15-18)*

The divine commission is not to seek out demonic forces. The commission is to go and spread the Gospel--casting out demons and overcoming spiritual serpents that you encounter along the pathway of duty as you continue to follow in the shadow of the Almighty.

Know what to do in case of snakebite. In case of an actual snakebite, an anti-venom should be administered as soon as possible. Spiritually, this is a great illustration of the work of the cross of Jesus Christ in freeing you from the poison infused by the venom of sin. If you have experienced a spiritual snakebite, you need not succumb to it. Let the anti-venom of the blood of Jesus infuse your life and it will totally cleanse you from the deadly venom of sin.

The Serpent Is Under Your Feet

The great news is that, through Jesus Christ, you have authority over spiritual snakes--Satan and his entire host of demonic powers. In Genesis 3 when God pronounced a curse upon the serpent He said that his head would be bruised by the seed of the woman. The seed of the woman is Jesus Christ and the bruise is a prophetic reference to Him bruising Satan's head through His death on the cross of Calvary.

When Jesus bruised Satan's head, it was much like severing the head of a poisonous snake in the natural world. A snake's head can be severed from its body, but it is still able to bite for hours afterwards. It is documented that the heart of one snake whose head was severed kept beating for two days while its body continued to move!

Jesus severed the head of the serpent at Calvary, but Satan is still active in the world today. That is why Jesus declared, *"Behold, I give unto you power to tread on serpents and scorpions, and over all the power of the enemy: and nothing shall by any means hurt you" (Luke 10:19).* When the Apostle Paul was attacked by an actual snake, he simply shook it off into the fire (Acts 28:5). Whatever attack the enemy launches against you, just shake it off until the spiritual viper releases its venomous fangs!

Psalm 91:13 declares that you will tread upon the cobra and trample the serpent under foot because your feet are set securely on the path following in the shadow of the Almighty. Remain there, and you need not fear spiritual serpents along the pathway to your destiny.

SECTION FIVE
DIVINE PROMISES

"Because he has set his love upon Me,
therefore I will deliver him;
I will set him on high,
because he has known My name.
He shall call upon Me,
and I will answer him;
I will be with him in trouble;
I will deliver him and honor him.
With long life I will satisfy him,
and show him My salvation."

(Psalm 91:14-16)

Chapter Fifteen
Loving The Lord

"Because he has set his love upon Me,
therefore I will deliver him..."

From the inception of our study, we learned that the promises
of Psalm 91 are conditional and apply to those dwelling in the
secret place of the Most High and abiding under the shadow
of the Almighty.

You have learned how God delivers you from snares and
pestilence, that you have refuge under His wings, and that you
are protected by the shield and buckler of His truth. You are
assured that you need not be afraid of terrors, arrows,
pestilence, or destruction and that even though others around
you may fall, you can remain standing. You are promised
that you will not experience the reward of the wicked because
you are a true believer who lives in the secret place under the
shadow of Almighty God.

You learned that because you have made the Lord your
refuge, no evil will befall you, nor shall any plague come near
your dwelling place. You are assured that His angels have
charge over you to keep you in all your ways so that you can
be victorious over spiritual stones, serpents, and lions.

Now, as you study Psalm 91:14-16, you will discover seven
additional promises which involve two more conditions.
Because you have set your love upon Him and have known
His name, God promises:

-I will deliver him.
-I will set him on high.
-I will answer him when he calls.
-I will be with him in trouble.
-I will honor him.
-I will satisfy him with long life.
-I will show him my salvation.

God's promises are obligations He imposes upon Himself but, as you have learned, many of His promises are conditional in nature. For example, the possession of the promised land depended upon Israel's obedience in claiming it. God promised that He would drive out all of the ungodly nations in the territory. Scouts were sent to spy out the land but--sadly--the people believed the negative report of the ten and rejected the positive declarations of Joshua and Caleb. They refused to enter in and, as a result, an entire generation--with the exception of these two men--perished in the wilderness. The promise of their right to the land was unconditional. The promise of their possession of it was conditional upon their obedience.

After the death of Moses, Joshua was delegated to lead the new generation of Israelites into their promised land. This time, the people obeyed God and He fulfilled His promises to drive out the nations and give them the land:

> *And the Lord gave to Israel all the land which He had sworn to give their fathers, and they possessed it and dwelt in it. The Lord gave them rest round about, just as He had sworn to their fathers. Not one of all their enemies withstood them; the Lord delivered all their enemies into their hands. There failed no part of any good thing which the Lord had promised to the house of Israel; all came to pass. (Joshua 21:43-45)*

Not one promise failed to come to pass! When the people obeyed God's Word, He fulfilled His promises because...

> *God is not a man that He should tell or act a lie, neither the son of man that He should feel repentence of compunction [for what He has promised]. Has He said and shall He not do it? Or has He spoken and shall He not make it good? (Numbers 23:19)*

Every promise of God will be fulfilled when you obey its conditions and rise up to claim it because *"he is faithful that promised" (Hebrews 10:23).*

As you review this final group of promises in Psalm 91, let the words with which Joshua challenged Israel resound in your soul: *"How long will you be slack to go in and possess the land which the Lord, the God of your fathers, has given you?"* The question isn't "When will God fulfill His promises?" The question is, "When will you meet the conditions necessary to possess them?"

This chapter discusses the first condition and promise *"Because he has set his love upon Me, therefore I will deliver him.."* The remaining promises will be discussed in following chapters.

Setting Your Love Upon God

Other translations of this verse read as follows:

> *-because he cleaves to me in love (RSV)*
> *-because he clings to me (NAB)*
> *-because he holds fast to me in love (ESV)*
> *-because he is lovingly devoted to Me...*
> *(Holman Bible)*

The first and greatest commandment is that you love God passionately:

> *And thou shalt love the Lord thy God with all thy heart, and with all thy soul, and with all thy mind, and with all thy strength: this if the first commandment. (Mark 12:30)*

To set your love upon Him means that by an act of your will, you pursue a deep love relationship with God to *"follow after righteousness, godliness, faith, love, patience, and meekness" (1 Timothy 6:11).*

You are to be rooted and grounded in love:

> *That Christ may dwell in your hearts by faith; that ye, being rooted and grounded in love, May be able to comprehend with all saints what is the breadth, and length, and depth and height; And to know the love of Christ which passeth knowledge, that ye might be filled with all the fullness of God.*
> *(Ephesians 3:17-19)*

Your work for the Lord is to be done as a labor of love, not as an imposed duty:

> *Remembering without ceasing your work of faith and labour of love... (1 Thessalonians 1:3)*

> *For God is not unrighteous to forget your work and labour of love, which ye have shewed toward His name, in that ye have ministered to the saints, and do minister. (Hebrews 6:10)*

Your passionate love for God is to flow through you to others:

*Jesus said unto him, Thou shalt love the Lord thy God
with all thy heart, and with all thy soul, and with all
thy mind. This is the first and great commandment.
And the second is like unto it, Thou shalt love thy
neighbour as thyself. On these two commandments
hang all the law and the prophets.
(Matthew 22:37-40)*

The entire revelation of God's Word hinges upon loving God
and others.

There are several different Greek words used for love. There
is *eros l*ove, which is the physical love between a man and a
woman which arises out of passion. The second Greek word
for love is *storge* love, representing feelings that exist
between a parent and a child or citizens and their benevolent
ruler. The third kind of love is *phileo* love which is relational
love like that between a husband and wife, brothers and
sisters, and dear friends. It is a love that cherishes and holds
someone or something dear to one's heart.

The love of which Psalm 91 speaks, however, is *agape* love
which is the highest form of love. It is a selfless and
sacrificial love that permeates your mind, reason, and will.
This kind of love can be experienced only if a person knows
God personally and receives His *agape* love into his life. It
was *agape* love that caused God to send His Son to die for
your sins. When you experience this kind of unconditional,
selfless love, then you will love God passionately and be able
to extend that same love to others.

To set your love upon God is to love Him with *agape* love, to
fix your heart, soul, mind--your entire being--upon God. It is
to cleave to Him with longing and delight. He does not
become a part of your life, He *is* your life. Your love is no
longer focused on the transitory things of the world. You set

your love upon God with a strong determination to never let anything or anyone interfere with it or rival it.

Deliverance Is Yours

You already studied deliverance in chapter 5 which focused on the first use of the word in Psalm 91 *"...surely He shall deliver thee" (Psalm 91:3)*. Here, in verse 14, God reassures you again that He stands ready to deliver and He repeats this once more in verse 15. Because you dwell in the secret place, abide under the shadow of the Almighty, and have set your love upon Him, He will deliver you. You don't have to wonder about it. You don't have to question it. He will deliver you!

Don't think that God is not honoring His promises just because your deliverance is not immediate. Job probably wanted deliverance on the first day of his terrible trial (Job 1), but it did not come for some time. The Psalmist was frequently admonishing God to make haste to help him (Psalm 70:1). Their deliverance eventually came, as will yours!

The Apostle Paul speaks of the past, present, and future dimensions of deliverance, declaring that God *"...delivered us from so great a death, and doth deliver: in whom we trust that he will yet deliver us..." (2 Corinthians 1:10)*.

Paul also declares with assurance, *"And the Lord shall deliver me from every evil work, and will preserve me unto his heavenly kingdom: to whom be glory for ever and ever." (2 Timothy 4:18)*. The Apostle Peter adds that *"the Lord knoweth how to deliver the godly out of temptations..." (2 Peter 2:9)*.

As we near the end of time here on earth, the love of many will not endure: *"And because iniquity shall abound, the love of many shall wax cold" (Matthew 24:12).* This means people will lose their love for God and others. Despite these negative circumstances, you have the assurance that nothing can separate you from God's love:

> *Who shall separate us from the love of Christ? shall tribulation, or distress, or persecution, or famine, or nakedness, or peril, or sword?... For I am persuaded, that neither death, nor life, nor angels, nor principalities, nor powers, nor things present, nor things to come, Nor height, nor depth, nor any other creature, shall be able to separate us from the love of God, which is in Christ Jesus our Lord.*
> *(Romans 8:35, 38-39)*

Because you love God, He not only wants to deliver you but He wants to set you on high because you have known His name--and that is the subject of the next chapter.

Chapter Sixteen
Knowing God's Name

"I will set him on high
because he has known my name."

The next promise in Psalm 91 is found in the latter portion of verse 14: *"I will set him on high because he has known my name."* The questions we will consider in relation to this verse are:

> -What does it mean to be set on high?
> -What does it mean to really know God's name?

Set On High

The Apostle Paul declared of Jesus:

> *...When he ascended up on high, he led captivity captive, and gave gifts unto men. (Now that he ascended, what is it but that he also descended first into the lower parts of the earth? He that descended is the same also that ascended up far above all heavens, that he might fill all things.)*
> *(Ephesians 4:8-10)*

When Jesus departed from this earth, He ascended into the presence of *"...the Lord our God, who dwelleth on high" (Psalm 113:5)*. The Heavenly Father dwells on high, Jesus ascended on high, and God wants to set you on high out of reach of all of your enemies.

In 2 Samuel chapter 22, David praises God for being delivered from his enemies:

And David spake unto the Lord the words of this song in the day that the Lord had delivered him out of the hand of all his enemies, and out of the hand of Saul...And that bringeth me forth from mine enemies: thou also hast lifted me up on high above them that rose up against me: thou hast delivered me from the violent man. (2 Samuel 22:1 and 49)

David was set on high above all his enemies--and that is exactly what God wants to do for you. God does not want you weighed down by the negative circumstances of life. The Apostle Paul said that we should know...

...what is the exceeding greatness of his power to usward who believe, according to the working of his mighty power, Which he wrought in Christ, when he raised him from the dead, and set him at his own right hand in the heavenly places, Far above all principality, and power, and might, and dominion, and every name that is named, not only in this world, but also in that which is to come: And hath put all things under his feet, and gave him to be the head over all things to the church, Which is his body, the fulness of him that filleth all in all.
(Ephesians 1:19-22)

The same power that raised Christ from the dead and set Him on high is the power that is resident within you because of the new birth experience:

But God, who is rich in mercy, for his great love wherewith he loved us, Even when we were dead in sins, hath quickened us together with Christ, (by grace ye are saved;) And hath raised us up together, and made us sit together in heavenly places in Christ

Jesus: That in the ages to come he might shew the exceeding riches of his grace in his kindness toward us through Christ Jesus. (Ephesians 2:4-7)

God wants to raise you up over every circumstance of life so you can sit in heavenly places with Jesus Christ. You are raised up together with Him! But once again, there is a divine stipulation to this promise: *"I will set him on high **because** he has known my name."* Other translations of this verse read:

> *-because he knows my name, from me he shall have protection (Knox)*
> *-I will set him securely on high (NAS)*
> *-Because he knows and understands my name. (AMP)*

The Prophet Habakkuk declared:

> *The Lord God is my strength, and he will make my feet like hinds' feet, and he will make me to walk upon mine high places. To the chief singer on my stringed instruments. (Habakkuk 3:19)*

In this verse, the prophet anticipates the restoration of God's people, proclaiming that they would once more rejoice in the mountains of Judea. What God did for them He will do for you. He will lift you up above the enemy, make your feet like hind's feet, and you will walk in the high places above your enemies and your adversities.

God's Name

Psalm 91:14 emphasizes knowing God's name, but it does not mean knowing it intellectually or casually. It means knowing His name spiritually, understanding the multi-faceted, intimate meanings of His names, and recognizing the divine power resident in them.

The word "know" is a term used in the Bible to describe an intimate relationship between a man and a woman. God wants you to know Him intimately. To enable you to do this, He has revealed various facets of His names which reflect His attributes and how He wants to relate to you.

You don't develop this kind of knowing by just showing up at church once in awhile or having a "Jesus" sticker on the bumper of your car. It only happens when you passionately desire, as did the Apostle Paul, to know Him *"in the power of his resurrection and the fellowship of His sufferings" (Philippians 3:10).* You learned the importance of confessing His name when you studied Psalm 91:1. Now you will learn more about the power of God's name and incorporate that knowledge into your spiritual life.

In many modern cultures, a name is simply a personal label used to distinguish people from one another. In Bible times, however, great significance was attached to a person's name. A name was often determined by some circumstance at the time of birth (1 Samuel 4:21). Sometimes a person's name expressed a hope or a prophecy (Isaiah 8:1-4; Hosea 1:4). Because of the importance of names in Bible times, God changed the names of several people. He changed Abram's name to Abraham in view of his destiny as the father of nations (Genesis 17:5). God also changed Sarai's name to Sara and changed Jacob's name to Israel for spiritual reasons. In the New Testament, this same pattern continued. Simon is called Peter, and Saul becomes Paul. Their name changes reflected their divine destinies in God's plan.

The names of God the Father, His Son Jesus Christ, and the Holy Spirit reveal their attributes and the ways in which they relate to believers. There is great power in these names, and this is why it is important for believers to know these names and their meanings.

The Names Of God

As we learned, Psalm 91 begins with the revelation of four different Hebrew names for God:

> *He that dwelleth in the secret place of **the Most High** shall abide under the shadow of **the Almighty.** I will say of **the Lord**, He is my refuge and my fortress: **my God**; in him will I trust. (Psalm 91:1-2)*

The Most High, the Almighty, the Lord, and my God: These four Hebrew names reveal who God is and what He wants to be in your life. He is the only God (the Most High) and the provider of all of your needs (the Almighty). He is the covenant keeper (the Lord) and the strong one (my God).

Subsequent revelations in scripture introduce what are referred to as the compound names of God. The name "Jehovah" means Lord, and the Bible combines this with other names of God to reveal His major attributes:

-Jehovah-Rapha:
 The Lord that heals: Exodus 15:26.
 -Jehovah-Nissi:
 The Lord our banner: Exodus 17:8-15.
 -Jehovah-Shalom:
 The Lord our peace: Judges 6:24.
 -Jehovah-Ra'ah:
 The Lord my shepherd: Psalms 23:1.
 -Jehovah-Tsidkenu:
 The Lord our righteousness: Jeremiah 23:6.

-Jehovah-Jireh:
  The Lord who provides: Genesis 22:14.
-Jehovah-Shammah:
  The Lord is there: Ezekiel 48:35.

The name "El" stands for the name "Elohim" and is used in combination with other descriptive titles for God:

-El Shaddai:
  The God who is sufficient for the needs of His people: Exodus 6:3.
-Elolam: The everlasting God: Genesis 21:33.
-El Elyon:
  The Most High God, exalted above all others: Genesis 14:18-20.
-Elohim: Used where the creative power of God is implied: Genesis 1:1.

In the Hebrew language in which the Old Testament was written, the word "Yahweh" means God. This word is combined with other descriptive titles to reveal more about the character of God.

-Yahweh Jireh:
  The Lord provides: Genesis 22:14.
-Yahweh Nissi:
  The Lord is my banner: Exodus 17:15.
-Yahweh Shalom:
  The Lord is peace: Judges 6:24.
-Yahweh Sabbaoth:
  The Lord of Hosts: 1 Samuel 1:3.
-Yahweh Maccaddeshcem:
  The Lord your Sanctifier: Exodus 31:13.
-Yahweh Roi:
  The Lord my shepherd: Psalms 23:1.

-Yahweh Tsidkenu:
The Lord our righteousness: Jeremiah 23:6.
-Yahweh Shammah:
The Lord is there: Ezekiel 48:35.
-Yahweh Elohim Israel:
The Lord God of Israel: Judges 5:3.

Additional names of God are:

-Quadosh Israel: The Holy One of Israel: Isaiah 1:4.
-Abba: Father: John 1:12-13.
-Adonai: Lord or Master: Isaiah 10:16,33.

Each of these names provide a deeper knowledge of who God is and what He wants to be in your life. God's name is not just a label. His names are expressions of His nature and identity. God says He will set you on high because you know His name. Take time to study the references listed by each name so you can come to know His names and their meanings.

The Name Of Jesus

The names of Jesus are also powerful because the Father and Son are one:

Jesus saith unto him, Have I been so long time with you, and yet hast thou not known me, Philip? he that hath seen me hath seen the Father; and how sayest thou then, Shew us the Father? Believest thou not that I am in the Father, and the Father in me? the words that I speak unto you I speak not of myself: but the Father that dwelleth in me, he doeth the works Believe me that I am in the Father, and the Father in me: or else believe me for the very works' sake.
(John 14:9-11)

209

To know God is to know Jesus, and to know Jesus is to know God. Regarding the name of Jesus, the Bible reveals that:

> *...God also hath highly exalted Him, and given Him a name which is above every name: That at the name of Jesus every knee should bow, of things in Heaven, and things in earth, and things under the earth; And that every tongue should confess that Jesus Christ is Lord, to the glory of God the Father. (Philippians 2:9-11)*

The name Jesus, meaning "Savior", was given to the Son of God when He came to earth in human form. He is also called Christ, which means "anointed one". These names are also combined into the titles of the Lord Jesus Christ, Jesus Christ, Christ Jesus, and Lord Jesus. Jesus is also called Emmanuel, which means "God with us." Jesus called Himself the Son of Man and He is often called the Son of God in New Testament writings. John calls Him the Word and the Lamb of God.

There is tremendous power in the name of Jesus. Merely chanting His name repeatedly is little more than a ritual, however, and can become vain repetition. The name of Jesus is not some magical phrase. You must have faith in the power inherent in His name. The disciples emphasized this after a tremendous healing recorded in Acts 3 when Peter said, *"...And His name through faith in His name hath made this man strong" (Acts 3:16).*

The Bible teaches that...

His name is powerful for salvation. The name of Jesus is the power of salvation from sin (Matthew 1:21; Acts 4:12; John 3:18).

His name is powerful for sanctification. Sanctification results from the power of God which is manifested in your life after salvation to enable you to live righteously (1 Corinthians 6:11).

His name is powerful in prayer. When you pray in His name and in harmony with His will, you receive what you ask (John 16:23-24).

His name is powerful in ministry. When Jesus departed for Heaven He declared, "*All power is given unto me in Heaven and in earth. Go ye therefore, and teach all nations, baptizing them in the name of the Father, and of the Son, and of the Holy Ghost; Teaching them to observe all things whatsoever I have commanded you: and, lo, I am with you alway, even unto the end of the world*" *(Matthew 28:18-20).*

His name is powerful in all you do. When you do something in the name of Jesus, even a simple task of serving is transformed into a powerful spiritual experience. You can sweep the church floors in the name of Jesus. You can prepare food for your family in the name of Jesus. You can work on an assembly line. What you do is not as important as how you do it and for whom you do it. Are you doing it well and in the name of Jesus? (Colossians 3:17).

Here is a list of the names of Jesus. Study and meditate on each reference so you can come to know the power in His name:

-Adam (the second): 1 Corinthians 15:45-47
-Advocate: 1 John 2:1
-Almighty: Revelation 1:8
-Alpha and Omega: Revelation 21:6
-Amen: Revelation 3:14
-Ancient of Days: Daniel 7:9

211

-Angel of His Presence: Isaiah 63:9
-Anointed Above His Fellows: Psalms 45:7
-Anointed (His): Psalms 2:2
-Apostle of our profession: Hebrews 3:1
-Arm of the Lord: Isaiah 51:9-10
-Author and Finisher of Faith: Hebrews 12:2
-Author of Eternal Salvation: Hebrews 5:9
-Beginning and end: Revelation 21:6
-Begotten of God: 1 John 5:18
-Beloved: Ephesians 1:6
-Bishop of Souls: 1 Peter 2:25
-Blessed and Only Potentate: 1 Timothy 6:15
-Branch (The): Zechariah 3:8
-Branch (Righteous): Jeremiah 33:15
-Branch of Root Of Jesse: Isaiah 11:1
-Bread of Life: John 6:48
-Bright and Morning Star: Revelation 22:16
-Captain of the Lord's Host: Joshua 5:15
-Carpenter's Son: Matthew 13:55
-Chief Cornerstone: 1 Peter 2:6
-Chief Among 10,000: Song of Solomon 5:10
-Chief Shepherd: 1 Peter 5:4
-Christ (The): John 1:41
-Christ the Lord: Luke 2:11
-Christ Jesus Our Lord: Romans 8:39
-Christ the Power of God: 1 Corinthians 1:24
-Counselor: Isaiah 9:6
-Covenant of the People: Isaiah 42:6
-Dayspring: Luke 1:78
-Daystar: 2 Peter 1:19
-Deliverer: Romans 11:26
-Door (The): John 10:9
-Elect: Isaiah 42:1
-Emmanuel: Matthew 1:23
-Eternal Life: 1 John 5:20
-Everlasting Father: Isaiah 9:6

-Faithful and True: Revelation 19:11
-Faithful Witness: Revelation 1:5
-First Begotten: Hebrews 1:6
-First Born: Psalms 89:27
-First Born Among Many: Romans 8:29
-First Fruits: 1 Corinthians 15:23
-First and Last: Revelation 22:13
-Foundation Laid in Zion: Isaiah 28:16
-Glorious Lord: Isaiah 33:21
-God of Israel: Isaiah 45:15
-God with Us: Matthew 1:23
-Great God: Titus 2:13
-Great High Priest: Hebrews 4:14
-Guardian of Souls: 1 Peter 2:25
-Head of the Body: Colossians 1:18
-Head over all Things: Ephesians 1:22
-Headstone of the Corner: Psalms 118:22
-Heir of all Things: Hebrews 1:2
-Holy One of Israel: Isaiah 41:14
-Hope of Glory: Colossians 1:27
-Horn of Salvation: Luke 1:69
-I Am: John 8:58
-Image of the Invisible God: Colossians 1:15
-Immanuel: Isaiah 7:14
-Jesus Christ Our Lord: Romans 1:3
-Judge of Israel: Micah 5:1
-King of Glory: Psalms 24:7
-King of Israel: John 12:13
-King of Kings: Revelation 17:14
-King: Zechariah 9:9
-King Over all the Earth: Zechariah 14:9
-Lamb of God: John 1:29
-Life: John 14:6
-Light of the World: John 8:12
-Lily of the Valley: Song of Solomon 2:1
-Living Bread: John 6:51

-Living Stone: 1 Peter 2:4
-Lord God Almighty: Revelation 4:8
-Lord and Savior: 2 Peter 2:20
-Lord of All: Acts 10:36
-Lord of Lords: Revelation 17:14
-Lord our Righteousness: Jeremiah 23:6
-Lord (Your Redeemer): Isaiah 43:14
-Lord Jesus Christ: 1 Peter 1:3
-Love: 1 John 4:8
-Man of Sorrows: Isaiah 53:3
-Master: Matthew 23:10
-Messiah: Daniel 9:25
-Mighty God: Isaiah 9:6
-Mighty One of Jacob: Isaiah 60:16
-Most Holy: Daniel 9:24
-Most Mighty: Psalms 45:3
-Nazarene: Matthew 2:23
-Only Wise God: 1 Timothy 1:17
-Our Passover Lamb: 1 Corinthians 5:7
-Physician: Luke 4:23
-Prince of Peace: Isaiah 9:6
-Prince of Kings of the Earth: Revelation 1:5
-Propitiation: Romans 3:25
-Rabbi: John 1:49
-Redeemer: Isaiah 59:20
-Resurrection: John 11:25
-Righteous Servant: Isaiah 53:11
-Rock: 1 Corinthians 10:4
-Root of Jesse: Isaiah 11:10
-Rose of Sharon: Song of Solomon 2:1
-Ruler: Matthew 2:6
-Savior of the World: 1 John 4:14
-Seed of David: John 7:42
-Seed of the Woman: Genesis 3:15
-Shepherd (good): John 10:11
-Son of God: Romans 1:4

-Son of Man: Acts 7:56
-Son of Mary: Mark 6:3
-Son of the Highest: Luke 1:32
-Star out of Jacob: Numbers 24:17
-Stone: Matthew 21:42
-Sun of Righteousness: Malachi 4:2
-Sure Foundation: Isaiah 28:16
-Teacher: John 3:2
-Truth: John 14:6
-Unspeakable Gift: 2 Corinthians 9:15
-Vine: John 15:1
-Way: John 14:6
-Wonderful: Isaiah 9:6
-Word: John 1:14
-Word of God: Revelation 19:13

Names Of The Holy Spirit

The names and titles of the Holy Spirit reveal much about His position and function as the third person of the Trinity of God. The Holy Spirit is called:

The Spirit of God: *Know ye not that ye are the temple of God, and that the Spirit of God dwelleth in you? (1 Corinthians 3:16)*

The Spirit of Christ: *But ye are not in the flesh, but in the Spirit, if so be that the Spirit of God dwell in you. Now if any man have not the Spirit of Christ, he is none of His. (Romans 8:9)*

The Eternal Spirit: This means the Holy Spirit is everlasting, with no beginning and no end: *How much more shall the blood of Christ, who through the eternal Spirit offered Himself without spot to God, purge your conscience from dead works to serve the living God? (Hebrews 9:14)*

The Spirit of Truth: *Howbeit when He, the Spirit of truth, is come, He will guide you into all truth: for He shall not speak of Himself; but whatsoever He shall hear, that shall He speak; and He will show you things to come. (John 16:13)*

The Spirit of Grace: *Of how much sorer punishment, suppose ye, shall he be thought worthy, who hath trodden under foot the Son of God, and hath counted the blood of the covenant, wherewith he was sanctified, an unholy thing, and hath done despite unto the Spirit of grace. (Hebrews 10:29)*

The Spirit of Life: *For the law of the Spirit of life in Christ Jesus hath made me free from the law of sin and death. (Romans 8:2)*

The Spirit of Glory: *If ye be reproached for the name of Christ, happy are ye: for the Spirit of glory and of God resteth upon you. (1 Peter 4:14)*

The Spirit of Wisdom and Revelation: *That the God of our Lord Jesus Christ, the Father of glory, may give unto you the Spirit of wisdom and revelation in the knowledge of Him. (Ephesians 1:17)*

The Comforter: The Holy Spirit comforts believers in times of trouble, sorrow, and loneliness: *But the Comforter, which is the Holy Ghost, whom the Father will send in my name... (John 14:26)*

The Spirit of Promise: The Holy Spirit is the Spirit of promise because He was sent to fulfill the promise given by Jesus, who...*being assembled together with them, commanded them that they should not depart from Jerusalem, but wait for the promise of the Father, which saith, ye have heard of me.*

For John truly baptized with water; but ye shall be baptized with the Holy Ghost not many days hence. (Acts 1:4-5)

The Spirit of Holiness: *And declared to be the Son of God with power, according to the Spirit of holiness, by the resurrection from the dead. (Romans 1:4)*

The Spirit of Faith: *We having the same spirit of faith, according as it is written, I believe and therefore have I spoken; we also believe, and therefore speak.*
(2 Corinthians 4:13)

The Spirit of Adoption: It is through the Holy Spirit that we are adopted into the family of God as the children of God: *For ye have not received the spirit of bondage again to fear; but ye have received the Spirit of adoption, whereby we cry, Abba, Father. (Romans 8:15)*

The Bible also uses several emblems to represent the Holy Spirit including a dove indicating peace and approval (John 1:32); oil indicating the anointing (Hebrews 1:9); water indicating cleansing and life (Isaiah 44:3); a seal showing ownership (Ephesians 1:13; 4:30; 2 Corinthians 1:22); wind which represents power (Acts 2:1-2); and fire indicating purification and passion (Exodus 3:2; 13:21; Isaiah 6:1-8).

Each of these names and emblems of the Holy Spirit yield tremendous insights into the inherent power of His name.

Lifted On High

The meaning of the names of God the Father, Jesus Christ, and the Holy Spirit make it evident as to how you can be lifted high above every circumstance of life and all the powers of the enemy.

Study the meaning of each name, pray using the appropriate name for your requests, and apply these names to your circumstances. For example, if you are in financial need, declare the name of Jehovah-Jireh, the Lord who provides. If your mind is in turmoil, declare His name Jehovah-shalom, the Lord of peace.

David declared, *"And they that know thy name will put their trust in thee: for thou, Lord, hast not forsaken them that seek thee" (Psalm 9:10).*

Through the Prophet Isaiah, God promised... *"Therefore my people shall know my name..." (Isaiah 52:6).*

By the word of Jeremiah God declared, *"And I will give them an heart to know me, that I am the Lord: and they shall be my people, and I will be their God: for they shall return unto me with their whole heart" (Jeremiah 24:7).*

When you really come to know God's name and its supernatural inherent power, He will set you on high above all your enemies. Proverbs 18:10 reveals that *"The name of the Lord is a strong tower: the righteous run into it, and are safe."* There, in the strong tower of God's name, you will be safe and secure from all of the attacks of the enemy.

So, now that you really know the power available to you through God's names it is time for you to...

> *...Arise [from the depression and prostration in which circumstances have kept you--rise to a new life]! Shine (be radiant with the glory of the Lord), for your light has come, and the glory of the Lord has risen upon you! (Isaiah 60:1, AMP)*

Chapter Seventeen
Receiving Answers From God

"He shall call upon me,
and I will answer him."

When one mentions calling someone in this modern technological society, a person most often thinks of placing a telephone call.

When you call a person by phone, your call may or may not be answered. You might be routed to voice mail or an answering machine or the line may be busy. Sometimes, when you contact a business by telephone, a recording may direct you to "Press 1 for Mrs. Smith, Press 2 for Mrs. Jones," etc.

One of the most amazing promises of Psalm 91 for those living in the secret place and abiding in God's shadow is that they can call upon God and He will answer. You won't be put on hold, You won't be routed to voice mail. The line won't be busy. God will answer your call.

Calling Upon God

Calling upon God is one of many terms used in the Bible to describe prayer which--simply put--is communicating with God. You may call upon God while standing (1 Kings 8:22; Mark 11:25); bowing down (Psalms 95:6); kneeling (2 Chronicles 6:13; Psalms 95:6; Luke 22:41; Acts 20:36); falling on your face (Numbers 16:22; Joshua 5:14; 1 Chronicles 21:16; Matthew 26:39); spreading out your hands (2 Chronicles 6:13); or lifting up your hands (Psalms 28:2;

Lamentations 2:19; 1 Timothy 2:8). Your position is not important. It is your calling that gets God's attention.

Prayer is described as calling upon the Lord in Genesis 12:8. Other references describe prayer as:

-Crying unto God:	Psalms 27:7; 34:6
-Drawing near to God:	Psalms 73:28
-Looking up:	Psalms 5:3
-Lifting up the soul:	Psalms 25:1
-Lifting up the heart:	Lamentations 3:41
-Pouring out the heart:	Psalms 62:8
-Pouring out the soul:	1 Samuel 1:15
-Crying to Heaven:	2 Chronicles 32:20
-Beseeching the Lord:	Exodus 32:11
-Seeking God:	Job 8:5
-Seeking the face of the Lord:	Psalms 27:8
-Making supplication:	Jeremiah 36:7

How Your Call Is Answered

Prayer is communication and a one-way conversation does not last long. When you call on God, expect Him to speak to you. The promise is, *"He shall call upon me, and I will answer him."*

God usually answers through His written Word or by a still small voice that seems to speak to your heart. Sometimes He will give you a vision or interpret back to your spirit what you have prayed in your heavenly prayer language.

God's answers include help in time of trouble, answers to your questions, guidance, and assistance in ordering your priorities. He doesn't say the answer will always come right at the moment you call--although it very well may. The Bible reveals that prayer is answered:

-Immediately at times: Isaiah 65:24; Daniel 9:21-23
-Delayed at times: Luke 18:7
-Different from our desires: 2 Corinthians 12:8-9
-Always beyond our expectations: Jeremiah 33:3

Jesus identified three levels of intensity in prayer: Asking, seeking, and knocking:

> *Ask, and it shall be given you; seek, and ye shall find; knock, and it shall be opened unto you: For every one that asketh receiveth; and he that seeketh findeth, and to him that knocketh it shall be opened.*
> *(Matthew 7:7-8)*

Asking is the first level of prayer. It is simply presenting a request to God and receiving an immediate answer. In order to receive, the condition is to ask: *"...ye have not, because ye ask not" (James 4:2).*

Seeking is a deeper level of prayer where answers are not as immediate as at the asking level. The account of the 120 believers gathered to pray in the upper room is an example of seeking. These men and women sought fulfillment of the promised infilling of the Holy Spirit and continued seeking until the answer came (Acts 1-2).

Knocking is a deeper level of prayer that is persistent and continues when answers are longer in coming. It is illustrated by the parable Jesus told in Luke 11:5-10 of a persistent caller seeking help from his friend. It is also illustrated by Daniel who continued to "knock" persistently during many days of spiritual battle when Satan tried to hinder the answer (Daniel 10:12-13).

As a believer abiding in the secret place, you are assured that when you call upon God you will receive an answer. The answer may be yes, no, or wait. His timing will be perfect, and even though the answer may be delayed or different than what you desired it will always be best for you and will always exceed your expectations.

Promises To Answer

In addition to the promise in Psalm 91:15, the scriptures contain many other assurances that God answers His people when they call.

The Psalmist said, *"In the day of my trouble I will call upon thee: for thou wilt answer me" (Psalm 86:7)* and declared *"As for me, I will call upon God; and the Lord shall save me" (Psalm 55:16).* He was assured that *"The Lord is nigh unto all them that call upon him, to all that call upon him in truth" (Psalm 145:18).*

The psalmist boldly declared, *"In the day of my trouble I will call upon thee: for thou wilt answer me" (Psalm 86:7)* and he determined that *"Because he hath inclined his ear unto me, therefore will I call upon him as long as I live" (Psalm 116:2).*

Through the psalmist, God promised: *"...And call upon me in the day of trouble: I will deliver thee, and thou shalt glorify me" (Psalm 50:15).* Through the Prophet Jeremiah, God declared: *"Call unto me, and I will answer thee, and shew thee great and mighty things, which thou knowest not" (Jeremiah 33:3).*

The Apostle John confidently declared, *"And whatsoever we ask, we receive of him, because we keep his commandments, and do those things that are pleasing in his sight" (1 John*

3:22) and "...this is the confidence that we have in him, that, if we ask any thing according to his will, he heareth us: And if we know that he hear us, whatsoever we ask, we know that we have the petitions that we desired of him" (1 John 5:14-15). Here are some of the powerful promises Jesus made regarding prayer:

> *Jesus answered and said unto them, Verily I say unto you, If ye have faith, and doubt not, ye shall not only do this which is done to the fig tree, but also if ye shall say unto this mountain, Be thou removed, and be thou cast into the sea; it shall be done. And all things, whatsoever ye shall ask in prayer, believing, ye shall receive. (Matthew 21:21-22)*

> *And whatsoever ye shall ask in my name, that will I do, that the Father may be glorified in the Son. If ye shall ask any thing in my name, I will do it. (John 14:13-14)*

> *If ye abide in me, and my words abide in you, ye shall ask what ye will, and it shall be done unto you. (John 15:7)*

> *Ye have not chosen me, but I have chosen you, and ordained you, that ye should go and bring forth fruit, and that your fruit should remain: that whatsoever ye shall ask of the Father in my name, he may give it you. (John 15:16)*

Unanswered Calls

Is it ever possible for a call to God to go unanswered? The answer is yes. God told Jeremiah not to pray for His sinful, rebellious people, because He would not hear his prayers (Jeremiah 7:16).

God may graciously answer the prayer of an unbeliever--and of course He always responds to prayer asking for salvation-- but the promises in Psalm 91 are guaranteed only to those dwelling in the secret place.

Review the verses in the previous paragraphs and you will find that the promises of an answer are to those who keep His commandments, do the things that are pleasing in His sight, and ask according to His will. When you are walking in the shadow of God, you will be doing what is pleasing in His sight and your requests will be in harmony with His will.

Jesus said you will receive answers to your prayers when God's Word abides in you (John 15:7) and He emphasized that you must have faith and not doubt (Matthew 21:21-22). James declares, *"But let him ask in faith, nothing wavering. For he that wavereth is like a wave of the sea driven with the wind and tossed. For let not that man think that he shall receive any thing of the Lord" (James 1:6-7).*

In discussing answers to prayer, the entire revelation of scripture must be taken into account. Your answer may be hindered by:

-Sin of any kind:	Isaiah 59:1-2; Psalm 66:18
-Idolatry:	Ezekiel 14:1-3
-An unforgiving spirit:	Mark 11:25; Matthew 5:23
-Selfishness, wrong motives:	Proverbs 21:13; James 4:3
-Manipulative prayers:	James 4:2-3
-Wrong treatment of a spouse:	1 Peter 3:7
-Self-righteousness:	Luke 18:10-14
-Unbelief:	James 1:6-7
-Not abiding in Jesus/the Word:	John 15:7
-Lack of compassion:	Proverbs 21:13
-Hypocrisy, pride, repetition:	Matthew 6:5

-Not asking according to God's will: James 4:2-3
-Not asking in Jesus' name: John 16:24
-Satanic demonic hindrances: Daniel 10:10-13
-Not seeking first the Kingdom: Matthew 6:33
-Not praying as you should: Romans 8:26

If you are a believer dwelling in the secret place and in the shadow of the Almighty and your answer doesn't seem to be coming when you call upon God, don't give up. Eliminate any of these hindrances to prayer and continue to ask, seek, and knock. Do not waver or doubt, or you will not receive from the Lord. Persist in your prayers, knowing that you will receive an answer in due season.

Never lose faith. Keep on calling on God because according to Psalm 91:15, He hears you and your answer is on the way--whether it be yes, no, or wait.

And His timing is always perfect.

Chapter Eighteen
Triumphing In Trouble

"I will be with him in trouble;
I will deliver him..."

Reading through Psalm 91, some believers have erroneously arrived at the conclusion that they will be immune to trouble because they are a born-again Christian. That is not what the scripture says. Psalm 91:15 declares, *"I will be with him in trouble..."* It does not say you will be kept *from* trouble, rather that God will be with you *in* trouble. It is not a matter of *if* you get in trouble, rather it is what God has promised to do *when* you are in trouble.

One of the promises given by Jesus was that *"In the world you shall have tribulation."* This is not a passage that is quoted very often as a favorite verse or treasured as a beloved promise. Nevertheless, it is a promise. Jesus assured that you would have tribulation, but then He added, *"...be of good cheer, I have overcome the world" (John 16:33).* The one who overcame the world, the one who lives within you because of your new birth experience--He is the one who stands ready to deliver you in troubled times. Because He overcame adversity, you too can overcome every troubling circumstance in your life.

You would not need help if you did not experience trouble, right? And that is the next part of the promise: *"...I will deliver him."* Other versions read *"I will be with him in hardship" (Har)* and *"in affliction, I am at his side" (Knox).* Literally it means, "as soon as trouble comes, I am there!" Young's Literal Translation says, *"I am with him in distress..."* The New International Reader's Version says, *"I will be with him in times of trouble..."* The Message Bible declares, *"'If*

*you'll hold on to me for dear life'," says God, 'I'll get you out
of any trouble. I'll give you the best of care if you'll only get
to know and trust me.'"*

When you face trouble, you do not face it alone. Whether the
trouble is your fault or not, God is right there with you. Israel
brought trouble on themselves many times during their
wilderness trek because of complaining, disobedience,
idolatry, and unbelief, yet God was still with them: *"But when
they in their trouble did turn unto the Lord God of Israel, and
sought him, he was found of them" (2 Chronicles 15:4).*

Read through Psalm 107 where Israel's history is summarized.
The people were frequently in trouble--much of which they
brought upon themselves. But repeatedly this chapter declares
that *"...they cried unto the Lord in their trouble, and he
delivered them out of their distresses" (Psalm107:6).*

Enough trouble will come your way in life that you don't need
to generate any more by making poor decisions. Your
decisions determine your destiny. Avoid bad decisions that
result in problems. Make good spiritual decisions. Make good
financial decisions. Don't hang out with the wrong people in
the wrong places. Flee temptation. Avoid trouble in every
way possible, but know that when you do encounter it--
whether it is your fault or not--God is with you, as He was
with Israel in the wilderness. Jesus said, *"...I will never leave
thee, nor forsake thee" (Hebrews 13:5).*

David proclaimed that the Lord was a refuge in troubled times
(Psalms 9:9) and that God would hide him in his pavilion--his
secret place (Psalms 27:5). It was in this hiding place that
David was preserved from trouble (Psalm 32:7). Throughout
the Psalms, David rejoiced that God knew of his adversities
and delivered him from them (Psalms 31:7; 54:7). He

proclaimed God as his strength in trouble (Psalms 37:39) and a very present help in times of need (Psalm 46:1).

David's key was that despite his trouble--whether it was his own fault or not--he always turned to God for help (Psalm 77:2). He called upon God in times of trouble, and God answered him (Psalm 81:7; 86:7). Because of this, David could boldly declare:

> *Though I walk in the midst of trouble, thou wilt revive me: thou shalt stretch forth thine hand against the wrath of mine enemies, and thy right hand shall save me. (Psalm 138:7)*

You may be walking in the midst of trouble today, but if you are following in God's shadow, He is right there with you. He is close enough to reach out His hand and deliver you.

King Solomon declared that the righteous are delivered out of trouble (Proverbs 11:8). Again, note that they are delivered *out* of it, not kept *from* it. The Prophet Nahum declared that the Lord was a stronghold in the day of trouble (Nahum 1:7). God promised through the prophet Isaiah:

> *When thou passest through the waters, I will be with thee; and through the rivers, they shall not overflow thee: when thou walkest through the fire, thou shalt not be burned; neither shall the flame kindle upon thee. (Isaiah 43:2)*

Talk about trouble! This passage is predicting floods and fire! Again, God does not say you will be kept from such things, but that you will go through them victoriously. The three Hebrews were not kept from the fiery furnace, but they were kept in it by one who appeared to bystanders to be the Son of God (Daniel 3:25).

Jesus said you should not let your heart--your innermost being--be troubled (John 14:1,27). The Apostle Paul declared, *"We are troubled on every side, yet not distressed; we are perplexed, but not in despair; Persecuted, but not forsaken; cast down, but not destroyed." (2 Corinthians 4:8-9).* There may be times in the midst of your trouble when you are distressed and perplexed, but you need not despair. You may be forsaken and cast down, but you won't be destroyed. God promised to be with you in trouble and deliver you out of it.

Nothing--no kind of trouble--can separate you from God when you remain in your spiritual secret place, abiding in His shadow:

> *Who shall separate us from the love of Christ? Shall tribulation, or distress, or persecution, or famine, or nakedness, or peril, or sword? As it is written, For thy sake we are killed all the day long; we are accounted as sheep for the slaughter. Nay, in all these things we are more than conquerors through him that loved us. For I am persuaded, that neither death, nor life, nor angels, nor principalities, nor powers, nor things present, nor things to come, Nor height, nor depth, nor any other creature, shall be able to separate us from the love of God, which is in Christ Jesus our Lord. (Romans 8:35-39)*

In all things--every kind of trouble--you are not only victorious, you are more than a conqueror through Jesus Christ.

I Will Deliver Him

This is the second time in Psalm 91 that God promises deliverance. In verse three is the promise that *"Surely he shall deliver thee from the snare of the fowler, and from the noisome pestilence."* As you studied this passage, you learned that part of Christ's divine mandate was to preach deliverance to captives (Luke 4:18). You also learned that Jesus ministered to those in bondage to the enemy and commissioned His followers to do likewise (Mark 16:15-17).

Psalm 91 guarantees that because you love God and know His name, He will be with you in trouble and deliver you. The Apostle Paul speaks of a past, present, and future dimension of deliverance, declaring that God *"...delivered us from so great a death, and doth deliver: in whom we trust that he will yet deliver us..." (2 Corinthians 1:10).*

Paul also declares with assurance, *"And the Lord shall deliver me from every evil work, and will preserve me unto his heavenly kingdom: to whom be glory for ever and ever." (2 Timothy 4:18).* The Apostle Peter adds that *"...the Lord knoweth how to deliver the godly out of temptations..."(2 Peter 2:9),*

Where Is God?

When Psalm 42 was written, David was experiencing a difficult time of trouble and he cried out:

> *As the hart panteth after the water brooks, so panteth my soul after thee, O God. My soul thirsteth for God, for the living God: when shall I come and appear before God? My tears have been my meat day and night, while they continually say unto me, Where is thy God? (Psalm 42:1-3)*

"Where is God?"--that is the question many ask in times of trouble. Where was God when my loved one died? Where was God when my mate left me? Where was He when my business failed? What about the tornado, the hurricane, the accident: Where was God?

David wrestled with that same question. Because of his adversities, he felt spiritually empty. He longed for God's presence. People around him were taunting him asking, "Where is your God?" Exiled from Jerusalem, in the midst of trouble, David made the mistake of looking back on the "good old days":

> *When I remember these things, I pour out my soul in me: for I had gone with the multitude, I went with them to the house of God, with the voice of joy and praise, with a multitude that kept holyday.*
> *(Psalm 42:4)*

David was remembering previous times in Jerusalem when he went to the temple with a multitude, joyfully praising God. He was comparing those days to his present situation in exile. This caused him to feel abandoned and forgotten by God as wave after wave of trouble passed over him:

> *I will say unto God my rock, Why hast thou forgotten me? why go I mourning because of the oppression of the enemy? (Psalm 42:9)*

In times of trouble, don't look back to the "good old days." Life may never be the same because of your trouble, but it will get better. Yesterday ended last night. Forget those things behind--whether good or bad--and look to the future.

David was greatly oppressed by the enemy. He was weeping (Psalm 42:3) and mourning (42:9), yet in the midst of his despair and through his tears, David encouraged himself in the Lord. He spoke to his own soul saying, *"Why art thou cast down, O my soul? and why art thou disquieted in me? hope thou in God: for I shall yet praise him for the help of his countenance" (Psalm 42:5).*

David offered a sacrifice of praise to God saying, *"Yet the Lord will command his lovingkindness in the daytime, and in the night his song shall be with me"...(verse 8).* Again in verse eleven he declared, *"Why art thou cast down, O my soul? and why art thou disquieted within me? hope thou in God: for I shall yet praise him, who is the health of my countenance, and my God."*

When you are troubled and in despair, speak words of encouragement to yourself. Remember what you learned in this study about the importance of your confession (chapter three) and how speaking God's Word activates the angels (chapter twelve).

Holocaust survivor Elie Wiesel wrote a book entitled *"The Night"* which was an account of his incarceration in Auschwitz, one of the German death camps which was established to exterminate Jews during World War II. Wiesel tells the story of three Jewish men--one of them a young boy--who were hanged alongside one another in front of the other prisoners. The inmates were all required to file past them and stare into their faces as they hung there. The two adult men died quickly, but the young boy weighed so little that he remained alive for some time. Mr. Wiesel recalls:

> *"For more than half an hour he stayed there, struggling between life and death, dying in slow agony under our eyes. We had to look at him full in the face. He was still alive when I passed in front of him, his tongue was still red, his eyes were not yet glazed. Behind me I heard a man asking, 'Where is God now?' And I heard a voice within me answer*

him, 'Where is He? Here He is! He is hanging here
on the gallows'."

As long as you live in this sinful world, you will experience trouble--hopefully not as horrible as the circumstances experienced by Mr. Wiesel. You are not immune to trouble, but as a believer who is following in God's shadow, when trouble comes He is right there with you.

Where was God when you were in trouble? He was right there with you honoring His promise. God did not--nor will He ever--abandon you.

Trusting God In Troubled Times

Trusting God is not hard in good times. True trust is best exhibited in troubled times, when everything goes wrong in your life. The Old Testament example of a man named Job is one of the greatest illustrations of trusting in troubled times. Read the tragic account of his story in Job 1-2 before proceeding with this chapter.

There are two things common to all people of every nation. They are common factors no matter where you live, what color your skin, or what language you speak. The first is that sin is present in every society. The Bible clearly indicates that all men have sinned and are in need of a Savior (Romans 3:23). The second common factor is that people everywhere experience unexplained trouble and suffering because of the presence of sin in the world.

We do not like to talk about suffering. We do not hear a great deal of preaching on this subject. We prefer to hear messages on victory and prosperity, and these things are good, as they are a great part of the revelation of God. But the Bible is not just a book of promises concerning the abundant life. It is a record of suffering, both of the righteous and the unrighteous.

We avoid the subject of suffering because there are elements involved in it that we do not understand and cannot explain. In this technological age, it seems everything must be understood and logically explained. When trouble comes, however, there are usually plenty of questions and often a scarcity of answers.

When Jesus was here on earth and spoke of the suffering He was to face on the cross, many of His followers deserted Him (John 6:55-66). They had expected their Messiah to reign in power and glory. Instead, He spoke of suffering and dying. They could not understand this, so they turned away. If you do not know how to trust God in times of trouble, you may also turn away from following Him when you face suffering.

According to Job 1-2, God's testimony of Job was that he was a righteous man who lived his life to please Him. Job did not suffer because he had sinned, as his friends claimed. They believed if Job repented, his circumstances would change. We must be careful when we view the suffering of others that we do not accuse them of sin, faithlessness, or unbelief. The Bible does teach that a sinful man reaps a bitter harvest because of sowing in fleshly corruption, but sowing and reaping cannot explain the suffering of the innocent.

Some people would say it was a terrible accident that the roof fell in and killed Job's children. They would blame the Chaldean forces for seizing his herds. They would attribute Job's skin infection to allergies or a virus. But there are no accidents in the lives of believers. Our world is not out of control. God is sovereign over every circumstance.

We often deny the sovereignty of God by our thoughtless comments."Tough luck," we say. "How unfortunate. What a tragic accident." If God is truly sovereign--and the Bible confirms that He is--it means He is in control. There is no luck, no fortune, or accident. He directs your life and limits all that touches you.

The first important truth evident in Job's trouble was that behind the scenes in the spiritual world was the true cause of Job's circumstances. There was a spiritual battle going on over his heart, mind, and allegiance. It was also a battle between the spiritual forces of Heaven and Hell, good and evil, truth and deception.

There is a battle going on in the spiritual world over you also and that warfare is most often manifested in the difficult circumstances you experience in the natural world. In times of trouble, continue to trust God, remembering that behind every natural circumstance you face there is always a spiritual cause.

The second important truth evident in Job's suffering is that, as a believer, nothing can enter your life without God's knowledge. Suffering may be inflicted by Satan, but its limits are set by God (Job 1:12).

Job was a wealthy man with many blessings, but he lost everything during this spiritual battle. Sometimes all that a man has is in the hands of Satan. Then the question is raised, will you serve God on the basis of who He is rather than what you receive from Him? Will you still serve God if there are no benefits attached? Will you serve Him simply because He is God? Some believers have what has been termed "consumer Christianity". They serve God for the perceived benefits and then turn away from Him when it seems like they aren't getting anything out of it.

When you fail to trust God, you will murmur and complain about your trouble as the nation of Israel did (Exodus 15:24). Complaining is different from honest questioning. Your murmuring is actually against God who is taking all of the circumstances of your life, both bad and good, and using them to accomplish His purposes:

> *And we know that all things work together for good to them that love God, to them who are the called according to His purpose. For whom He did foreknow, He also did predestinate to be conformed to the image of His Son, that He might be the firstborn among many brethren. (Romans 8:28-29)*

God is using every circumstance to conform you to His image. When you complain about any of these difficulties, you are in reality complaining against God and His work in your life.

If you are not trusting God in times of trouble, you may become discouraged and depressed as did the Prophet Jeremiah who lamented:

> *...My strength and my hope is perished from the Lord; Remembering mine affliction and my misery, the wormwood and the gall. My soul hath them still in remembrance, and is bowed in me.*
> *(Lamentations 3:18-20)*

Focusing on your troubles results in despair, depression, and discouragement. In troubled times, always remember that you do not face your difficulties alone. If friends fail, finances vanish, and your cherished plans are aborted, Jesus is right there with you in the midst of the circumstances. The Bible confirms that "...*in all our afflictions, He was afflicted*" *(Isaiah 63:9)*.

When you place your trust in God in troubled times, your focus is changed from temporal problems to eternal benefits:

> *For our light affliction, which is but for a moment, worketh for us a far more exceeding and eternal weight of glory; While we look not at the things which are seen, but at the things which are not seen; for the things which are seen are temporal; but the things which are not seen are eternal.*
> *(2 Corinthians 4:17-18)*

God works in your affliction when you focus on the eternal benefits rather than the affliction itself. Trials and problems in life are not unusual or without purpose:

> *Beloved, think it not strange concerning the fiery trial which is to try you, as though some strange thing happened unto you: But rejoice, inasmuch as ye are partakers of Christ's sufferings; that, when His glory shall be revealed, ye may be glad also with exceeding joy. (1 Peter 4:12-13)*

Coming To Know God

It was through his troubles that Job came to know God more intimately and see himself more clearly. He never received an answer to all of his questions, and if he had there would have been no room for faith because it is the "substance of things not seen." At the end of his time of suffering Job declared:

I have heard of thee by the hearing of the ear: but now mine eye seeth thee. Wherefore I abhor myself and repent in dust and ashes. (Job 42:5-6)

Some of us have only a secondhand knowledge of God. When we are experiencing the blessings of life, we sometimes consider God a luxury rather than a necessity. But when you have a real need, God becomes a necessity. Job came to know God more intimately through his trouble. Before he suffered, Job knew God through theology. Afterwards, he knew Him by experience.

Paul expressed a similar desire when he said:

That I may know Him, and the power of His resurrection and the fellowship of His sufferings, being made conformable unto His death.
(Philippians 3:10)

We only come to know God in resurrection power through the intimate fellowship of suffering which comes into our lives through troubling circumstances. The Apostle Paul spoke of a time of trouble in his life, explaining that *"... we would not, brethren, have you ignorant of our trouble which came to us in Asia, that we were pressed out of measure, above strength, insomuch that we despaired even of life: But we had the sentence of death in ourselves, that we should not trust in ourselves, but in God which raiseth the dead"* (2 Corinthians 1:8-9).

The word "trouble", as used in this passage, speaks of extremely heavy pressure, like a rock being lowered upon a victim and slowly crushing the life out of him. Paul's trouble was without measure, meaning it was beyond the normal range of difficulties. It was excessive to the extent that Paul despaired, thinking there was no way out. He felt he wasn't going to make it through, believing he had the sentence of death hanging over his life. But Paul did make it through this difficult time and because of this experience he and his missionary team learned to trust in God rather than themselves. What will you learn from your time of trouble?

Throughout his suffering, Job questioned God as to the cause of his troubles. It is not wrong to question God. Jesus knew the purpose for which He had come into the world was to die for the sins of all mankind, yet in His hour of suffering He cried out, "*My God, My God, why hast thou forsaken me* " It is what follows the questioning that is important. His next words were, "*Into thy hands I commit my spirit.*"

Despite his many questions and fruitless discussions with his friends, Job's bottom-line response was... "*Though He slay me, yet will I trust in Him...*" *(Job 13:15).* He also declared:

> *For I know that my Redeemer liveth, and that He shall stand at the latter day upon the earth: And though after my skin worms destroy this body, yet in my flesh shall I see God. (Job 19:25-26)*

After all your questioning is finished, the emphasis must change from *me* to *Thee*. You must commit your trouble and suffering, with all the unanswered questions, into the hands of God.

You have questions when you experience trouble because you think you must understand something in order to accept it. But lack of understanding does not prevent good coming from that which you do not understand. You may not understand the principles of electricity when you switch on a light, yet you benefit from it.

When we face trouble, we often think we have a right to know why and that we would be able to understand if only the reasons were revealed to us. Both are incorrect premises. Knowing does not guarantee understanding and knowledge is not synonymous with acceptance. If you can totally understand a thing, you have mastered it. If you could totally understand all that God allows to touch your life, then you would become as God. The very first temptation of man focused on this desire when Satan said, "You shall be as gods and know..." Our problem is that we are still battling with our human reasoning by trying to explain with natural answers that which can only be discerned spiritually.

When you experience unexplained difficulties in your life, do you seek the answers or do you simply trust God? The Bible says, *"The secret things belong unto the Lord our God; but those things which are revealed belong unto us..." (Deuteronomy 29:29).* There are some secret things that belong only to the Lord. You may never understand the purposes of your trouble, but you do not have to seek desperately to find meaning. You do not have to justify the unexplained actions of God or man. Leave the secret things with the Lord.

Just because you do not see meaning to an event in the natural world does not mean there is no purpose for it spiritually. So, *"Since the Lord is directing our steps, why try to understand everything that happens along the way?" (Proverbs 20:24, The Living Bible).*

When God finally talked with Job, He used several examples from nature which Job could not explain. God emphasized that if Job could not understand what he saw in the natural world, he certainly could not understand what he could not see in the spiritual world.

When Job faced God at the end of his season of trouble, it no longer mattered that he did not get answers to his questions about suffering. He was in the direct presence of God, and that experience left no room for anything else. He was no longer controlled and tormented by human reasoning. He replaced questions, not with answers, but with trust.

God was with Job in his trouble and--true to His promises-- delivered him and blessed him once again:

> *So the Lord blessed the latter end of Job more than his beginning: for he had fourteen thousand sheep, and six thousand camels, and a thousand yoke of oxen, and a thousand she asses. He had also seven sons and three daughters...After this lived Job an hundred and forty years, and saw his sons, and his sons' sons, even four generations. So Job died, being old and full of days. (Portions of Job 42:12-17)*

Life after his season of trouble was never again the same. He had lost his first family, business, and home. But eventually there was supernatural restoration and multiplication. What God has for you in the future always exceeds the losses of your past.

Job learned to trust in troubled times. Paul learned to trust God in the midst of trouble. You will learn this lesson also, as God is with you in times of trouble. You may not have answers for all of the difficulties you have experienced in life, nor for those you may face in the future. But you can be assured of this: God is with you in trouble as long as you remain secure in your secret place in Him.

In every difficulty, a vital key to victory is to praise and worship God. When you face difficult times, maintain the attitude of the Prophet Habakkuk who declared:

Although the fig tree shall not blossom, neither shall fruit be in the vines; the labour of the olive shall fail, and the fields shall yield no meat; the flock shall be cut off from the fold, and there shall be no herd in the stalls: Yet I will rejoice in the Lord, I will joy in the God of my salvation. The Lord God is my strength, and he will make my feet like hinds' feet, and he will make me to walk upon mine high places.
(Habakkuk 3:17-19)

The Bible commands, *"In everything give thanks: for this is the will of God in Christ Jesus concerning you"* (1 Thessalonians 5:18). God doesn't say for you to hypocritically give thanks *for* everything, rather you are to give thanks *in* everything. In spite of it all. In the midst of it all!

Right now, lift your hands to the Lord and give Him praise, despite your trouble and in the midst of your trouble. You are not alone. He is right there with you in your secret place to strengthen and sustain you. Your yesterday ended last night and your future will be better than your past.

"For I know the plans I have for you," declares the Lord, "plans to prosper you and not to harm you, plans to give you hope and a future."
(Jeremiah 29:11, NIV)

Chapter Nineteen
Being Honored By God

"I will...honor him."

We come to an interesting statement in Psalm 91 in verses 14-15 which promises *"...because he has set his love upon Me, ...I will honor him."* You may be thinking, "I thought honor was something we give to God, our parents, and our spiritual leaders."

...And you are right. As believers, we are to honor God: *"Now unto the King eternal, immortal, invisible, the only wise God, be honour and glory for ever and ever"* *(1 Timothy 1:17)*.

We are to honor Jesus: *"That all men should honour the Son, even as they honour the Father" (John 5:23)*.

We are to honor our parents: *"Honour thy father and thy mother: that thy days may be long upon the land which the Lord thy God giveth thee" (Exodus 20:12)*.

We are also instructed to honor our leaders:

> *Let every soul be subject unto the higher powers. For there is no power but of God: the powers that be are ordained of God. Whosoever therefore resisteth the power, resisteth the ordinance of God: and they that resist shall receive to themselves damnation...For he is the minister of God to thee for good. But if thou do that which is evil, be afraid; for he beareth not the sword in vain: for he is the minister of God, a revenger to execute wrath upon him that doeth*

245

evil...For for this cause pay ye tribute also: for they are God's ministers, attending continually upon this very thing. Render therefore to all their dues: tribute to whom tribute is due; custom to whom custom; fear to whom fear; honour to whom honour. (Portions of Romans 13:1-7)

While it is true that we are to give honor to God and those to whom the Bible says it is due, Psalm 91 reveals that God will honor the ones who dwell in the secret place, abide in His shadow, set their love upon Him, and come to know His name. These are the prerequisites for claiming this promise.

Seeking Honor

We all want to be esteemed by others. We seek approval from our peers and loved ones, and we all struggle with rejection from time to time. But consider this question: Are you more concerned about being honored by man or by God?

A man named Haaman sought the honor of man and ended up dying on a gallows (Esther 6-7). King Saul was more concerned about receiving honor from the elders and the people than repenting of his sin against God (1 Samuel 15:30).

Jesus questioned, *"How can ye believe, which receive honour one of another, and seek not the honour that cometh from God only?" (John 5:44).* The people Jesus was addressing were more concerned about their status and position in the eyes of man than receiving honor from God.

The disciples in the early church got it! They declared, *"We ought to obey God rather than men."* They knew that affirmation from God is more important than the approval of man (Acts 5:29). If you seek honor from man, you become

246

man-controlled. If you seek honor from God, you become God-controlled. Which is more important--having your life and ministry honored and controlled by God or being honored and controlled by man?

Being Honored By God

So how can you be honored by God? First, you must recognize that the source of true honor is not man, your boss, your peers, your family, or the media. God is the source of true honor:

> *Both riches and honour come of thee, and thou reignest over all; and in thine hand is power and might; and in thine hand it is to make great, and to give strength unto all. (1 Chronicles 29:12)*

In Psalm 91, honor is promised to those who fulfill certain requirements. Dwelling in the secret place is the first prerequisite because *"Glory and honour are in his presence; strength and gladness are in his place" (1 Chronicles 16:27).* Abiding in God's shadow, loving Him, and knowing His name are the other requirements which culminate in the fulfillment of this promise from God.

Elsewhere in scripture, God says, *"...for them that honour me I will honour, and they that despise me shall be lightly esteemed" (1 Samuel 2:30).* If you honor God, He will honor you.

If you follow Jesus, you will be honored by God:

> *If any man serve me, let him follow me; and where I am, there shall also my servant be: if any man serve me, him will my Father honour. (John 12:26)*

247

Applying Biblical wisdom and godly understanding in your life results in honor:

> *Wisdom is the principal thing; therefore get wisdom: and with all thy getting get understanding. Exalt her, and she shall promote thee: she shall bring thee to honour, when thou dost embrace her.*
> *(Proverbs 4:7-8)*

Listening to wise instruction and reproof brings honor:

> *Poverty and shame shall be to him that refuseth instruction: but he that regardeth reproof shall be honoured. (Proverbs 13:18)*

Humility leads to honor because *"Before destruction the heart of man is haughty, and before honour is humility"* *(Proverbs 18:12)* and *" By humility and the fear of the Lord are riches, and honour, and life" (Proverbs 22:4).*

True honor also results from living righteously: *"He that followeth after righteousness and mercy findeth life, righteousness, and honour" (Proverbs 21:21)* and from doing good works: *"But glory, honour, and peace, to every man that worketh good..." (Romans 2:10).*

Living In Divine Favor

To be honored by God is to live in His divine favor. Let's look at a few people mentioned in scripture as being favored of the Lord.

The Bible records that Noah found favor with God (Genesis 6:8). Joseph was favored and blessed with prophetic dreams and interpretations (Genesis 39:6). Israel was granted supernatural financial favor when they left slavery, taking with them the treasures of Egypt (Exodus 12:36).

Divine favor can bring the right companion into your life, as illustrated by the story of Ruth and Boaz in the book of Ruth. The three Hebrew young men were favored by God (Daniel 1:4) and Nehemiah obtained favor of the king to return to Jerusalem and rebuild the walls (Nehemiah 1). The angel told Mary, who was to be the mother of Jesus, that she was highly favored of the Lord (Luke 1:30).

From these examples, we learn that living in divine favor can provide protection, supernatural provision, bring a companion into your life, and enable the fulfillment of your divine destiny.

Interestingly enough, each of these people who found favor with God also went through great difficulties. Noah experienced ridicule while building the ark and he witnessed the destruction of the beautiful world and its inhabitants. Joseph was sold into slavery, falsely accused, and sent to prison. Israel faced a frightening situation at the Red Sea. Ruth experienced great loss and poverty before finding the favor of God through Boaz. The three Hebrew men mentioned in Daniel were cast into a furnace of fire because of the stand they took for God. Nehemiah faced ridicule and persecution as he labored to fulfill his vision. And Mary, who was to be the mother of Jesus, faced the possibility of death because in the eyes of society she was an unwed mother--an offense which carried the death penalty in those days.

What we discover in each of these examples is that living in God's divine favor and being honored by Him is not necessarily a life of pleasure and ease. Favor--being honored by God--can result in danger, difficulty, hardship, and persecution. But wouldn't you rather be honored by Him and do great things than simply go through life as a nominal believer who has secured little more than eternal "fire insurance" through their conversion?

Finding Favor

Favor does not result from knowing the right people to open doors, networking, being talented, or having money. Your family background, social, or economic status does not attract God's favor. The favor of God rests upon those who learn to abide in the divine dwelling of God in the secret place (Psalm 91:1).

Enduring trials victoriously results in God's honor resting upon you:

> *Wherein ye greatly rejoice, though now for a season, if need be, ye are in heaviness through manifold temptations: That the trial of your faith, being much more precious than of gold that perisheth, though it be tried with fire, might be found unto praise and honour and glory at the appearing of Jesus Christ.*
> *(1 Peter 1:6-7)*

When you are honored by God, you must live with integrity. Just one act of folly can ruin your reputation: *"Dead flies cause the ointment of the apothecary to send forth a stinking savour: so doth a little folly him that is in reputation for wisdom and honour"* (Ecclesiastes 10:1). If you are known as a believer and a person of integrity, you need to live up to that honor. One unguarded moment, one stupid decision, one sinful act--and it can all be destroyed.

The Apostle Paul described in detail how to live life as a vessel of honor:

Nevertheless the foundation of God standeth sure, having this seal, The Lord knoweth them that are his. And, Let every one that nameth the name of Christ depart from iniquity. But in a great house there are not only vessels of gold and of silver, but also of wood and of earth; and some to honour, and some to dishonour. If a man therefore purge himself from these, he shall be a vessel unto honour, sanctified, and meet for the master's use, and prepared unto every good work. Flee also youthful lusts: but follow righteousness, faith, charity, peace, with them that call on the Lord out of a pure heart. But foolish and unlearned questions avoid, knowing that they do gender strifes. And the servant of the Lord must not strive; but be gentle unto all men, apt to teach, patient, In meekness instructing those that oppose themselves; if God peradventure will give them repentance to the acknowledging of the truth; And that they may recover themselves out of the snare of the devil, who are taken captive by him at his will. (2 Timothy 2:19-26)

According to this passage, to be a vessel of honor you must:
- Depart from iniquity.
- Flee lust.
- Follow righteousness, faith, charity, and peace.
- Call on the Lord out of a pure heart.
- Avoid foolish questions.
- Refuse to create or be part of strife.
- Be gentle to all men.
- Be apt (able) to teach and teachable.
- Be patient.
- Instruct those who oppose you in meekness.

If you set your love upon God and come to know Him intimately, then Psalm 91:14-15 promises that He will honor you.

The Prophet Daniel shared a simple formula for obtaining the favor of the Lord:

> *Just as it is written in the Law of Moses, all this disaster has come upon us, yet we have not sought the favor of the Lord our God by turning from our sins and giving attention to your truth. (Daniel 9:13, NIV)*

Turning from sin and giving attention to the truth of the Word are two vital keys for walking in divine favor.

In summary...

-You will either be a vessel of honor or dishonor.

-You will either live life striving for the approval of man or you will seek honor from God.

Which do you value most: The favor of God or the favor of man?

Chapter Twenty
Living A Satisfied Life

"With long life I will satisfy him..."

One of the promises made in Psalm 91 to those who abide in the secret place is that God will satisfy them with long life. People can live to be very old, but they may also grow bitter, resentful, and hateful. God doesn't want you just to live a long life. He wants you to live a satisfied, productive, and contented life.

The Darby Bible says, *"with length of days I will satisfy him..."* The Wylciff Bible says *"I shall fulfill him with the length of days".*

A Satisfied Life

First let's examine the word "satisfy" in this promise. As used here, the word means full and complete. God doesn't want you to live a life where you are only enduring your existence and barely surviving from day-to-day. He wants you to experience a full, complete, and satisfied life.

All of the material things that we think bring joy and satisfaction--houses, lands, cars, money, and other material possessions--can be gone in one moment through a calamity. This why Jesus declared, *"...a man's life consisteth not in the abundance of the things which he possesseth" (Luke 12:15).* Someday, the entire world and all of the material things in it will pass away (1 John 2:17).

Your possessions do not result in living a satisfied life and that is why your focus should not be on material things. Jesus said, *"Therefore I say unto you, Take no thought for your life, what ye shall eat, or what ye shall drink; nor yet for your body, what ye shall put on. Is not the life more than meat, and the body than raiment?" (Matthew 6:25).*

The life that satisfies comes only through Jesus Christ who said, *"...I am come that they might have life, and that they might have it more abundantly" (John 10:10)*. Jesus not only wants you to have life, but He wants you to have abundant life.

The entire revelation of scripture is written *"... that ye might believe that Jesus is the Christ, the Son of God; and that believing ye might have life through his name" (John 20:31)*. Jesus is the way, the truth, and the life (John 14:6). He is not *a* way of life. He is *the* life. Jesus is the spiritual bread and water of life that satisfies the deepest hunger and thirst of your soul and gives true meaning to your existence:

> *And Jesus said unto them, I am the bread of life: he that cometh to me shall never hunger; and he that believeth on me shall never thirst. (John 6:35)*

The bottom line is this simple: *"He that hath the Son hath life; and he that hath not the Son of God hath not life" (1 John 5:12)*. One of the saddest comments in scriptures is when Jesus said, *"And ye will not come to me, that ye might have life" (John 5:40)*.

You Will Live Forever

An abundant, satisfied life is only possible when you realize that through Christ you have eternal life: *"For the wages of sin is death; but the gift of God is eternal life through Jesus Christ our Lord" (Romans 6:23)*. How could you ever live a happy life if you believed that everything ends at death--that

254

you would cease to exist and you would never see your loved ones again? The Apostle Paul declared:

> *For if the dead rise not, then is not Christ raised: And if Christ be not raised, your faith is vain; ye are yet in your sins. Then they also which are fallen asleep in Christ are perished. If in this life only we have hope in Christ, we are of all men most miserable. But now is Christ risen from the dead, and become the firstfruits of them that slept. (1 Corinthians 15:16-20)*

Many people are unhappy because they think their present existence is all that there is to life. Paul said if you believe this, you will be "most miserable." Without the hope of eternal life, you will not live a satisfied life.

The scriptures are clear that true life--both now and eternally--comes only through Jesus Christ:

> *For God so loved the world, that he gave his only begotten Son, that whosoever believeth in him should not perish, but have everlasting life. (John 3:16)*

> *He that believeth on the Son hath everlasting life: and he that believeth not the Son shall not see life; but the wrath of God abideth on him. (John 3:36)*

> *Verily, verily, I say unto you, He that believeth on me hath everlasting life. (John 6:47)*

> *And this is life eternal, that they might know thee the only true God, and Jesus Christ, whom thou hast sent. (John 17:3)*

The major purpose of God's Word is the revelation that you can have life through Jesus Christ: *"But these are written,*

*that ye might believe that Jesus is the Christ, the Son of God;
and that believing ye might have life through his name"
(John 20:31).*

While it is true that the physical body you now possess will
someday cease to function, you will actually never die:

> *Jesus said unto her, I am the resurrection, and the
> life: he that believeth in me, though he were dead, yet
> shall he live... (John 11:25)*

If you have accepted Jesus Christ as Savior, you already have
everlasting life:

> *Verily, verily, I say unto you, He that heareth my
> word, and believeth on him that sent me, hath
> everlasting life, and shall not come into
> condemnation; but is passed from death unto life.
> (John 5:24)*

When you accepted Jesus, you passed from spiritual death to
spiritual life. You are already living eternal life right now! If
you are reading this page, then you are living it this side of
the grave. Someday, unless Jesus returns first, you will be
absent from your body and present with the Lord. You will
be living out your eternal life on the other side of the grave.
Paul said concerning this:

> *We are confident, I say, and willing rather to be
> absent from the body, and to be present with the Lord.
> (2 Corinthians 5:8).*

Paul was confident. There was no doubt. He knew that his
life would continue after death.

Living A Long Life

The promise of long life in Psalm 91:16 obviously includes the concept of eternal life. King David asked God for life and received *"length of days forever and ever" (Psalm 21:4)*. Although David knew his physical body would eventually die, he declared by faith: *"Thou wilt prolong the king's life: and his years as many generations. He shall abide before God for ever." (Psalm 61:6-7)*.

Let's take time to examine Psalm 91:16 further. Could this passage promising a long and satisfying life mean more than just eternal life?

Most of us have read Psalm 90:10 which states, *"The days of our years are threescore years and ten; and if by reason of strength they be fourscore years, yet is their strength labour and sorrow; for it is soon cut off, and we fly away."* Threescore and ten years is a total of 70 years and fourscore years means 80 years. Many of us have been taught, based on this passage, that we are blessed if we make it to age 70 and anything beyond that age is an unusual benefit.

But Psalm 90 was written after Israel rebelled against God and describes what happened because of His judgment for their sin:

> *For we are consumed by thine anger, and by thy wrath are we troubled. Thou hast set our iniquities before thee, our secret sins in the light of thy countenance. For all our days are passed away in thy wrath: we spend our years as a tale that is told. (Psalm 90:7-9)*

Are you still living under God's judgment? Not if you have accepted Jesus Christ as your Savior. Are you still struggling with the sins of your past? Not if you have repented and asked forgiveness. Are you going to die because of God's wrath, as did the disobedient Israelites who perished in the wilderness? If you are a true believer, absolutely not! So if verses 7-8 were directed to Israel and do not apply personally to you, why would you accept verse ten to limit your life to 70 or 80 years?

Psalm 90:10 is not a personal word of the Lord to believers. Yes, it is God's Word, and yes, it was true of the disobedient Israelites, but this is not a set span of lifetime imposed upon true believers. We are not Israel, we didn't turn our backs on God, and our children aren't waiting for us to die in order to enter their promised land.

Movies, television, and advertisements promote youth and make a person feel disposable with age. The enemy puts in your mind that at age 70 you are old and from then on you are living on borrowed time. But did you know that God originally created you to live a lot longer? Before man's original sin, of course, there was no death and no limit at all on life. After mankind fell into sin, God declared, "...My Spirit shall not strive with man forever, for he is indeed flesh; yet his days shall be one hundred and twenty years" (Genesis 6:3). God set 120 years as a life span--even after mankind's fall into sin. This means if you are 60 years old, you are just middle aged!

You may not live to be 120 years old, but what you need to eliminate is the thinking that your life is over at 70 or 80 years old. The psalmist declared, "...Mine age is as nothing before thee..."(Psalm 39:5). He said that "Those that be planted in the house of the Lord shall flourish in the courts of our God. They shall still bring forth fruit in old age; they shall be fat and flourishing" (Psalm 92:13-14).

258

At age 85, after forty years of difficult life in the desert wilderness, Caleb declared:

> *And now, behold, the Lord hath kept me alive, as he said, these forty and five years, even since the Lord spake this word unto Moses, while the children of Israel wandered in the wilderness: and now, lo, I am this day fourscore and five years old. As yet I am as strong this day as I was in the day that Moses sent me: as my strength was then, even so is my strength now, for war, both to go out, and to come in. Now therefore give me this mountain! (Joshua 14:10-12)*

Do you know how to tell when you are truly old? You are old when you no longer have a vision for God. The Bible says, *"...your young men shall see visions" (Acts 2:17)*. As long as you are receiving new visions from God, you are still young spiritually even if you are 100 years old!

It is when you start looking back instead of looking ahead that you grow old. The Apostle Paul declared:

> *Brethren, I count not myself to have apprehended: but this one thing I do, forgetting those things which are behind, and reaching forth unto those things which are before, I press toward the mark for the prize of the high calling of God in Christ Jesus. (Philippians 3:13-14)*

Paul wasn't sitting around reflecting on the good old days, nor was he lamenting over the terrible days when he persecuted the church. Paul was constantly pressing forward to fulfill his destiny. Get out of your retirement mentality! Start looking ahead and focusing on fulfilling your destiny in whatever time you have left, be it five years or fifty!

The Bible commands, *"Say not thou, What is the cause that the former days were better than these? for thou dost not inquire wisely concerning this" (Ecclesiastes 7:10)*. The Prophet Isaiah declared under the inspiration of the Holy Spirit, *"Remember ye not the former things, neither consider the things of old. Behold, I will do a new thing; now it shall spring forth; shall ye not know it? I will even make a way in the wilderness, and rivers in the desert" (Isaiah 43:18-19)*. As long as you are looking forward to new things, you will never truly grow old.

You can choose life! The Apostle Paul said:

> *For to me, to live is Christ, and to die is gain. But if I live on in the flesh, this will mean fruit from my labor; yet what I shall choose I cannot tell. For I am hard pressed between the two, having a desire to depart and be with Christ, which is far better. (Philippians 1:21-23)*

Paul had an intimate relationship with the Lord and longed to be with Him, but he also recognized the value of fulfilling his destiny here on earth. Paul said, *"What I shall choose, I cannot tell..."* Paul was in a bit of a dilemma when he penned these words, desiring to remain on earth and wanting to go to be with God at the same time. But Paul chose life until the time he could declare with certainty, *"I have fought a good fight, I have finished my course, I have kept the faith: Henceforth there is laid up for me a crown of righteousness, which the Lord, the righteous judge, shall give me at that day: and not to me only, but unto all them also that love his appearing" (2 Timothy 4:7-8)*. You, too, can choose to live a life that is long enough to fulfill your divine destiny.

Sara had faith that, despite her advanced age, God would be faithful to do what He had promised:

Through faith also Sara herself received strength to conceive seed, and was delivered of a child when she was past age, because she judged him faithful who had promised. (Hebrews 11:11)

Abraham did not consider his age a hindrance to receiving God's promises:

And being not weak in faith, he considered not his own body now dead, when he was about an hundred years old, neither yet the deadness of Sara's womb: He staggered not at the promise of God through unbelief; but was strong in faith, giving glory to God; And being fully persuaded that, what he had promised, he was able also to perform.
(Romans 4:19-21)

Zachariah and Elisabeth were quite elderly when Elisabeth became pregnant with John the Baptist:

And they had no child, because that Elisabeth was barren, and they both were now well stricken in years.
(Luke 1:7)

What new thing will you conceive and give birth to when you stop worrying about your advanced age?

Dying Young

Is it possible to die before your time?

[Although all have sinned] be not wicked overmuch or willfully, neither be foolish--why should you die before your time? (Ecclesiastes 7:17, AMP)

261

Willful sin and foolish decisions can lead to premature death. For example, if you jump off a high cliff it is a foolish act denying the laws of gravity set in place by God. As a result, you may die before your time. Ananias and Saphira, whose story is recorded in Acts chapter five, died before their time because of a sinful, foolish decision.

"What about true believers who die young?," you may ask. As a believer, you must realize that everything that happens isn't about you and your happiness, but it is about fulfilling your destiny and accomplishing God's plans and purposes.

The hall of faith in Hebrews 11 speaks of those who by *"...faith subdued kingdoms, wrought righteousness, obtained promises, stopped the mouths of lions, Quenched the violence of fire, escaped the edge of the sword, out of weakness were made strong, waxed valiant in fight, turned to flight the armies of the aliens."* (Hebrews 11:33-35).

But this chapter also speaks of those who were destitute, afflicted, tormented, and martyred as being men and women of faith. God wants to give you dying faith as well as living faith. He wants you to have an abundant life, live long enough to fulfill His purposes, and leave this world satisfied that you have fulfilled your destiny, whether you die young or old.

One of the greatest examples illustrating this occurred in January of 1956 when, after many months of planning, five missionaries prepared to contact the fierce Auca Indians of Ecuador.

Nate Saint, a missionary pilot, was going to fly the men to a place called Palm Beach, where they had previously made contact with the Aucas by dropping gifts to them from the air.

He and Jim Elliot, Pete Fleming, Ed McCully, and Roger Youderian collected what they would need for their mission.

Prior to their departure on January 3rd, the men sang one of their favorite hymns:

> *We rest on thee, our Shield and our Defender,*
> *Thine is the battle, thine will be the praise.*
> *When passing through the gates of pearly splendor,*
> *Victors, we rest with thee through endless days.*

Once on the beach, the men built a tree house and prepared to contact the Indians. On Friday, January 6, a visit from an Auca man and two women encouraged the missionary team. They spent several hours together and gave the man a ride in their plane.

Saturday, no natives appeared, but on Sunday morning when Nate flew over the site, he spotted some Auca men walking toward their beach. At 12:30 P.M. Nate made a prearranged radio call to his wife, Marj, back at the mission station: "Looks like they'll be here for the early afternoon service. Pray for us. This is the day! Will contact you at 4:30."

When 4:30 came, the missionary wives switched on the radio. Silence. Five minutes went by, then ten minutes, and then hours passed. Sundown came, and still no word.

Monday morning, January 9, 1956, Johnny Keenan, another missionary pilot, flew to the beach to try to make contact with the men. He reported that he found the plane on the beach with all of the fabric stripped off, but there was no sign of the men.

The radio station HCJB in Ecuador flashed the news to the rest of the world: "Five men missing in Auca territory."

Lieutenant General William K. Harrison, commander in chief of the Caribbean Command, himself a Christian, was contacted and by noon he had organized a ground party to go to the site.

On Wednesday, Keenan made his fourth flight over the beach and reported he had seen a body floating face down in the river. The search party eventually located four of the five bodies, but the body of Ed McCully was never found, having been swept away by the river. The other four men were buried on Palm Beach, seemingly a tragic, premature end to five promising young lives.

But was it the end? By 1958, Betty Elliot (wife of Jim Elliott) and Rachel Saint, (Nate Saint's sister) were living among the Auca Indians carrying on the missionary work. One-by-one, the Aucas put their faith in Jesus Christ. The five men who murdered the missionaries eventually became Christians and emerged as spiritual leaders among their people. After these men were believers, they shared how on the fateful day that they committed their murderous acts they heard singing from above the trees. Looking up they saw what appeared to be a canopy of bright lights as God welcomed the missionaries home. Nine years later, Nate Saint's children, Kathy and Stephen, were baptized at Palm Beach by two of the men who had killed their father.

But the story of these five young missionaries does not end there. Hundreds of young people were inspired by their deaths to accept the call of God to missions. Many veteran missionaries serving around the world today responded to the call because of the martyrdom of these young men.

These men lived long enough to fulfill their God-given destinies. Today, they live on in the lives of the Aucas who found Christ, the many who responded to the call of missions, and--of course--they live on in eternity. With long life, they are satisfied.

God wants to give you sufficient days to accomplish your divine destiny. When it is your time to die, He wants you to be satisfied--not only with the length of your years, but also that your work for God is completed. No matter what your age, you will be ready to depart and be joyfully looking forward to the eternal life that awaits you.

How To Extend Your Life

Do you think you can actually lengthen your life? Your immediate answer might be "No." But the Bible says you can! This does not mean you can overrule God's sovereignty, of course, for as you learned--life is not about you but about His purposes. Your times are in His hands (Psalm 31:15). But the Bible does reveal that you can extend your life by following scriptural principles that will keep you from physical and spiritual harm. Let's take a look at these:

Dwell in the secret place. If you dwell in the secret place and abide under the shadow of the Almighty, then God promises to satisfy you with long life.

Remain under His wings. Physical, mental, spiritual, and emotional healing are all "in His wings," so you should continue to abide under them if you want to extend your life (Malachi 4:2).

Keep God's commandments. Solomon admonished, *"My son, forget not my law; but let thine heart keep my commandments: For length of days, and long life, and peace, shall they add to thee" (Proverbs 3:1-2).*

Exercise Godly wisdom. *"Wisdom is the principal thing; therefore get wisdom: and with all thy getting get understanding...receive my sayings; and the years of thy life shall be many"* *(Proverbs 4:7 and 10).*

Listen to Godly instruction. *"Take fast hold of instruction; let her not go: keep her; for she is thy life"* *(Proverbs 4:13).*

Guard your heart and spirit. Solomon admonished, *"Keep thy heart with all diligence; for out of it are the issues of life"* *(Proverbs 4:23).* The issues of life flow from your heart. If you harbor bitterness, anger, or unforgiveness, it affects you physically, mentally, and spiritually. Worrying about the future also affects you negatively. This is why Jesus taught us to pray, *"give us this day our daily bread"*--meaning our daily needs. God structured the universe to run on the pattern of a single day. When you break that pattern by living in the past or future, negative emotions result that lead to an unfulfilled life and possibly even premature death. Proverbs 18:14 and 17:22 indicate that a wounded and broken spirit affects the physical body. Psalms 38 shows how sin is related to both physical and emotional conditions. Guard your heart and spirit and bring them under the control of the Holy Spirit.

Fear God. *"The fear of the Lord is the beginning of wisdom: and the knowledge of the holy is understanding. For by me thy days shall be multiplied, and the years of thy life shall be increased"* *(Proverbs 9:10-11).*

Control your tongue. You can speak words of death or life over yourself. The Bible says, *"Death and life are in the power of the tongue: and they that love it shall eat the fruit thereof"* *(Proverbs 18:21)* meaning you will live what you confess. Peter admonished, *"For he that will love life, and see good days, let him refrain his tongue from evil, and his lips that they speak no guile"* *(1 Peter 3:10).* Living a long and satisfied life is definitely related to controlling your tongue.

Seek first God's Kingdom.   When you seek first the Kingdom of God, all other things are added unto you (Matthew 6:33). "All other things" includes living a lengthy, satisfying life.

Give the Word priority in your life. God's Word is like medicine. It brings healing (Psalms 107:17-20), strength (Psalms 119:25-28), and life (John 6:32-33). If you give the Word priority in your life and walk in obedience to it, you will not commit sins that result in sickness and death-- conditions like sexually transmitted diseases and illnesses resulting from addiction to alcohol, tobacco, and drugs.

Treat your body as a temple.   It has been estimated by doctors that 60% of all illness results from an unhealthy lifestyle. The body is sacred because it is the temple of the Holy Spirit (1 Corinthians 3:16). Because your body is a temple, do not ingest toxic substances such as liquor, tobacco, or addictive drugs. Eat right and exercise from the motivation of living longer to fulfill your divine destiny rather than just to look good.

Live in peace.   Peter says if you love life and want to see good days, seek peace and pursue it (1 Peter 3:11, NKJV). Don't be a trouble-maker. Be a peace-maker. Avoid division and ungodly conflict.

Accept Jesus as your Healer. Just because you are a believer does not mean you are immune to sickness, but you can be healed of sickness and have your life extended. Jesus bore your sicknesses and carried your diseases at the same time He bore your sins (Matthew 8:17). The psalmist cautions that you should not forget His benefits, which include healing (Psalms

103:1-3). Sin and sickness are Satan's twin evils. Salvation and healing are God's twin provisions. Before Calvary, people were saved and healed by looking forward to the cross in faith. Afterwards, salvation and healing come by looking back by faith to Christ's work on the cross.

Did you accept Jesus only as Savior, or did you accept Him as Healer also? How can He keep you from sin if you have never accepted Him as Savior? How can He keep you from sickness if you have never accepted Him as Healer? In Romans 10:9, the word "saved" is the same word used by Mark when he said, that as many as touched Jesus were made whole. Salvation is divine deliverance from sin and its penalties, of which sickness is a part. The Greek word *"sozo"* carries the meaning of physical and spiritual healing. The only "surely" (a word of emphasis) in the redemption chapter of Isaiah 53 precedes His provision for our healing.

There is, of course, sickness unto death. The Prophet Elisha healed many people during his ministry, but there came a day that he was sick with the sickness from which he would die (2 Kings 13:14). He did not lose faith, because some time later when a dead man was thrown in on top of his bones, the man was resurrected (2 Kings 13:21). Elisha had more power in his dead bones than many living, breathing believers!

It's All About God

Remember that the length of your life and the condition of your physical body is not about you, but about God's purposes. Nearing his death, Moses was still strong and vital (Deuteronomy 34:7). Joshua was old and well-stricken in years (Joshua 23:2). Both of these men fulfilled God's purposes. Their physical conditions and years of life had nothing to do with living a satisfied life.

John the Baptist died in prison. Peter was delivered from prison. The difference was their divine purpose, not the level of their spirituality. John's work was finished. Peter's ministry was just starting.

Abraham was satisfied with his life when he died *"full of years"* (Genesis 25:8). He knew he had fulfilled his divine mandate. Joseph knew when his work on earth was done and told his family, *"I die."* Then he blessed his sons and grandchildren, gave a great prophetic mandate, and died (Genesis 50:24-26).

The scriptures say that David, *"after he had served his own generation by the will of God, fell asleep, and was laid unto his fathers..." (Acts 13:36).*

The Apostle Paul declared:

> *For I am now ready to be offered, and the time of my departure is at hand. I have fought a good fight, I have finished my course, I have kept the faith: Henceforth there is laid up for me a crown of righteousness, which the Lord, the righteous judge, shall give me at that day: and not to me only, but unto all them also that love his appearing.*
> *(2 Timothy 4:6-8)*

Paul viewed his forthcoming death in terms of a drink-offering being poured out to God. He saw it as a departure, like a ship hauling anchor and leaving port. He viewed it as a fighter who had won the war, as a runner who had finished the course, and as a good steward who had kept what was entrusted to him.

In the New Testament, a man named Simeon had received a promise through the Holy Spirit that he would not die before seeing the Lord Jesus Christ. When Mary and Joseph brought Jesus to the temple, the promise was fulfilled:

> *And, behold, there was a man in Jerusalem, whose name was Simeon; and the same man was just and devout, waiting for the consolation of Israel: and the Holy Ghost was upon him. And it was revealed unto him by the Holy Ghost, that he should not see death, before he had seen the Lord's Christ. And he came by the Spirit into the temple: and when the parents brought in the child Jesus, to do for him after the custom of the law, Then took he him up in his arms, and blessed God, and said, Lord, now lettest thou thy servant depart in peace, according to thy word: For mine eyes have seen thy salvation, Which thou hast prepared before the face of all people; A light to lighten the Gentiles, and the glory of thy people Israel. (Luke 2:25-32)*

When Simeon at last saw Jesus, he knew every promise God had given him had been fulfilled and he was ready to depart from this life in peace.

So let's wrap up the promise of a long and satisfying life with this summary:

> -When you truly know and love God, He will extend your life long enough to fulfill His purposes.

> -Whether you die young or old, you will be satisfied because you have achieved your divine destiny and every promise of God has been fulfilled in your life.

-You will have sufficiency of life in this world and eternal life in the world to come.

-You will depart this world with satisfaction, a sense of fulfillment, and great anticipation of the eternity that awaits you.

Chapter Twenty-One
Claiming The Benefits Of Salvation

"...I will show him My salvation."

To those who abide in the secret place and walk in the shadow of the Almighty, God promises to reveal His salvation. Here are the basic facts about salvation:

> -Salvation is by the grace of God: 2 Corinthians 6:1-2; Ephesians 2:5-8; 2 Timothy 1:9; Titus 2:11.

> -Salvation is available to all: 1 Timothy 2:4; Titus 2:11; 2 Peter 3:9; Romans 1:16.

> -It is God's desire that all be saved: 1 Thessalonians 5:9; 2 Peter 3:9.

> -Salvation is only available through Jesus Christ, God's Son, our Savior: Acts 4:12; 1 Thessalonians 5:9; 1 Timothy 1:15.

> -Salvation is received by grace through faith: Ephesians 2:8; 1 Peter 1:5.

> -Salvation is secured and confirmed by confessing and believing: Romans 10:9.

To be saved, you must hear the gospel, believe it, and act upon that knowledge by repenting from sin, calling on the name of the Lord, and confessing Him as Lord and Savior.

From what are you saved? The biblical doctrine of salvation reveals that you are saved from wrath, that is, from God's judgment (Romans 5:9). You are delivered from the sin which has separated you from God and from the consequence of that sin (Romans 6:23).

These are the basic truths of the Gospel, but there is much more about salvation that God wants to reveal to those who dwell in the secret place.

Benefits Of Salvation

The word "salvation" means to be rescued from a place of danger or death. Biblical salvation is being saved from sin and its consequence of spiritual death, but the benefits of salvation are much more than that.

The word "salvation", as used in the Bible, not only means spiritual redemption, but it refers to healing, deliverance, preservation, and protection. Salvation has many benefits, and that is the subject of this chapter as we focus on the final phrase in Psalm 91: *"I will...show him my salvation".*

An overview of scriptures reveals the following benefits of salvation. Take time to read each verse in your Bible and meditate on these benefits.

-We are foreknown by God:
 Acts 2:23; Romans 8:29; 1 Peter 1:2.
-We are chosen:
 Matthew 22:14; 1 Peter 2:4.
-We are called:
 1 Thessalonians 5:24.
-We are reconciled to God:
 Romans 5:10; 2 Corinthians 5:18-20; Colossians 1:20; Ephesians 2:14-17.
-We are redeemed from sin:
 Romans 3:24; Colossians 1:14; 1 Peter 1:18.

-We are delivered from condemnation:
 John 3:18; 5:24; Romans 8:1.
-We live under grace instead of judgment:
 Romans 3:24-26; 1 John 2:2.
-We are free from the law:
 Romans 7:4; 6:14; 2 Corinthians 3:11;
 Galatians 3:25.
-We are dead to the old sin nature and alive to God:
 Romans 6:8; Colossians 3:3; 1 Peter 2:24.
        -Buried with Him:
         Romans 6:4; Colossians 2:12.
        -Raised with Him:
         Colossians 3:1.
-We are children of God:
 Galatians 3:26; John 1:12; 2 Corinthians 6:18.
-We are a new creation:
 2 Corinthians 5:17; Galatians 6:15; Ephesians 2:10.
-We are adopted into the family of God:
 Romans 8:15; 8:23; Ephesians 1:5; 2:19;
 Galatians 6:10.
-We are justified and declared righteous:
 Romans 3:24; 5:1, 9; 8:30; 1 Corinthians 6:11;
 Titus 3:7.
-We are forgiven of sin:
 Ephesians 1:7; 4:32; Colossians 1:14; 2:13; 3:13.
-We are delivered from the kingdom of Satan:
 Colossians 1:13a; 2:15.
-We have citizenship in God's Kingdom:
 Luke 10:20; Ephesians 2:13,19; Philippians 3:20;
 Colossians 1:13b.
-We have a secure spiritual foundation:
 1 Corinthians 3:11; 10:4; Ephesians 2:20.
-We have access to God:
 Romans 5:2; Ephesians 2:18; Hebrews 4:14,16;
 10:19-20.

-We are heirs of God and joint-heirs with Christ:
Romans 8:17; Ephesians 1:14; Colossians 3:24;
Hebrews 9:15; 1 Peter 1:4.
-We are ambassadors, ministers, workers with God:
2 Corinthians 3:6, 9; 5:20; 6:4.
-We are recipients of eternal life:
John 3:15; 10:28; 20:31; 1 John 5:11-12.
-We are complete in Him:
Colossians 2:10.
-We are recipients of spiritual blessings:
Ephesians 1:3.
-We are:
> -Members of His Body: 1 Corinthians 12:13.
> -Branches in the Vine: John 15:5.
> -Stones in the building: Ephesians 2:21-22.
> -Sheep in the flock: John 10:27-29.
> -Part of His Bride: Ephesians 5:25-27.
> -Priests in the Kingdom: 1 Peter 2:9.

-We are recipients of the ministry of the Holy Spirit:
> -Born of the Spirit: John 3:6.
> -Baptized with the Spirit: Acts 1:5;
> 1 Corinthians 12:13.
> -Indwelled by the Spirit: John 7:39; Romans
> 5:5;8:9; 1 Corinthians 3:16; 6:19; Galatians
> 4:6.
> -Sealed by the Spirit: 2 Corinthians 1:22;
> Ephesians 4:30.
> -Given spiritual gifts: 1 Corinthians 12:11,
> 27-31; 13:1-2.

Loaded With Benefits

The Psalmist declared, *"Blessed be the Lord, who daily loadeth us with benefits, even the God of our salvation" (Psalm 68:19).* In Psalm 103, the psalmist enumerates some of these benefits:

Bless the Lord, O my soul: and all that is within me, bless his holy name. Bless the Lord, O my soul, and forget not all his benefits: Who forgiveth all thine iniquities; who healeth all thy diseases; Who redeemeth thy life from destruction; who crowneth thee with lovingkindness and tender mercies; Who satisfieth thy mouth with good things; so that thy youth is renewed like the eagle's. The Lord executeth righteousness and judgment for all that are oppressed. He made known his ways unto Moses, his acts unto the children of Israel. The Lord is merciful and gracious, slow to anger, and plenteous in mercy. He will not always chide: neither will he keep his anger for ever. He hath not dealt with us after our sins; nor rewarded us according to our iniquities. For as the heaven is high above the earth, so great is his mercy toward them that fear him. As far as the east is from the west, so far hath he removed our transgressions from us. Like as a father pitieth his children, so the Lord pitieth them that fear him. For he knoweth our frame; he remembereth that we are dust. As for man, his days are as grass: as a flower of the field, so he flourisheth. For the wind passeth over it, and it is gone; and the place thereof shall know it no more. But the mercy of the Lord is from everlasting to everlasting upon them that fear him, and his righteousness unto children's children; To such as keep his covenant, and to those that remember his commandments to do them. The Lord hath prepared his throne in the heavens; and his kingdom ruleth over all. Bless the Lord, ye his angels, that excel in strength, that do his commandments, hearkening unto the voice of his word. Bless ye the Lord, all ye his hosts; ye ministers of his, that do his pleasure. Bless

the Lord, all his works in all places of his dominion:
bless the Lord, O my soul. (Psalm 103)

"Bless the Lord," the psalmist exclaims, "and don't forget His benefits!" Then he proceeds to list some of these wonderful benefits:

-He forgives your iniquities.
-He heals your diseases.
-He redeems your life from destruction.
-He crowns you with loving-kindness and tender mercies.
-He satisfies your mouth with good things so that your youth is renewed like the eagle's.
-He is gracious, slow to anger, and plenteous in mercy.
-He executes righteousness and judgment.
-He does not deal with you or reward you according to your sins and iniquities.
-He removes your transgressions.
-He pities those who fear Him--meaning He shows you compassion.
-He knows you intimately.
-His mercy and righteousness extend to you, your children, your grandchildren, and to all who keep His covenant and commandments.
-His Kingdom rules over all the circumstances of your life.
-He has a host of angels who minister to you and fulfill His Word in your behalf.

God wants you to experience the unlimited lengths, breadths, depths, and heights of the benefits of His salvation.

What Shall We Do?

The psalmist was so overwhelmed by the tremendous benefits of salvation that he wondered how he could possible repay the Lord for His goodness. He questioned, *"How can I repay the Lord for all of His benefits to me?"* Then he answered his own rhetorical question by declaring:

> *I will lift up the cup of salvation and call on the name of the Lord. I will fulfill my vows to the Lord in the presence of all his people...O Lord, truly I am your servant; I am your servant, the son of your maidservant; You have freed me from my chains. I will sacrifice a thank offering to you and call on the name of the Lord I will fulfill my vows to the Lord in the presence of all his people, in the courts of the house of the Lord--in your midst, O Jerusalem. (Psalm 116:13-19, NIV)*

The psalmist said he would express his gratitude to God for the benefits of salvation by calling upon His name, paying his vows, serving Him, remaining free from the chains of sin, offering a sacrifice of thanksgiving, and honoring Him in the presence of the people. Take a few minutes to analyze each of these in terms of your own life.

Calling upon the Lord. The psalmist declared that he would call only upon the name of the Lord. This means he would not turn to idols, other people, or rely upon his own wisdom in difficult times. Who do you call upon when you have a need? Who do you turn to for help? When you call upon the name of the Lord you are expressing your confidence in the benefits of your salvation.

Paying vows. The psalmist said that he would pay his vows to the Lord. What have you promised God in times past? Have you honored those commitments?

Serving Him. The psalmist said, "I am your servant." Are you demonstrating a servant attitude in your ministry to others? Are you truly serving God?

Remaining free from sin. The psalmist said, "You have freed me from my chains." Are you walking in the liberty that salvation affords, or are you bound by legalism, addictions, habits, sin, and wrong attitudes? Walking in spiritual freedom is one of the greatest ways to honor God for the benefits of salvation.

Offering a sacrifice of thanksgiving. It is easy to offer thanks when everything is going great, but what do you do in difficult times? That is when offering thanks is a sacrifice because you don't feel thankful. No matter what you are going through today, take time right now to offer a sacrifice of thanksgiving. The benefits of salvation remain true, even in tough times.

Honoring God in the presence of the people. Some believers are what we might call "secret service Christians." They say their faith is a "private and personal matter." But the psalmist said that one of the ways to repay God for the benefits of salvation is to honor Him in the presence of the people. Do people know you are a believer? Do you honor God in their presence or do you participate in their ungodly conversations and laugh at their dirty jokes?

The closing phrase of Psalm 91 expresses God's desire to show the benefits of His salvation to those who dwell in the secret place, abide under the shadow of the Lord God Almighty, set their love upon Him, and know His name.

Conclusion
Remaining In His Presence

The promises you studied in Psalm 91 can only be fulfilled in your life when you become a true believer in God and are born-again through Jesus Christ. If you did not make this decision when you read the Introduction to this book, turn there right now, read it again, and follow the steps given to repent of your sins and accept Jesus as your Savior.

For believers, Psalm 91 contains many powerful promises, but there are conditions for receiving them. You must dwell spiritually in the right place--in the secret place of the Most High (verses 1 and 9). You must abide under the shadow of the Almighty (verse 1) and bring your confession into alignment with God's Word (verse 2). You must set your love upon God and come to know His name experientially (verse 14).

When you meet these requirements, God promises to deliver you, provide refuge under His wings, and protect you by the shield and buckler of His truth. You are assured that you need not fear the snare of the fowler, pestilence, terrors, arrows, destruction, plagues, and spiritual stones, lions, and snakes. This list is inclusive of every type of material, spiritual, or physical attack one could possibly experience!

As a believer, you are promised that even though others around you may fall, you can remain standing and that you will not experience the reward of the wicked. You are assured that the angels have charge over you to keep you in all your ways as you continue to walk in God's shadow.

God has also promised to deliver you when you are in trouble, set you on high above all your enemies, answer when you call, honor you, satisfy you with long life, and reveal to you the tremendous benefits of His salvation so that they can be manifested in your life.

God cannot lie. He will fulfill these promises. You can confidently place your hope in the pledges of Psalm 91 and anchor your soul to them (Hebrews 6:18-19).

These divine promises will enable you to escape the evil corruption of the world: *"Whereby are given unto us exceeding great and precious promises: that by these ye might be partakers of the divine nature, having escaped the corruption that is in the world..." (2 Peter 1:4)*

As possessors of these promises, let us take the Apostle Paul's advice that *"Having therefore these promises, dearly beloved, let us cleanse ourselves from all filthiness of the flesh and spirit, perfecting holiness in the fear of God" (2 Corinthians 7:1).*

If you remain in the secret place of God's presence, then when you near the conclusion of your time here on earth, you will be able to look back over your life and ministry and declare:

> *"Not a word failed of any good thing*
> *which the Lord had spoken*
> *...all came to pass."*
> *(Joshua 21:45, NKJV)*

Appendix
Translations Of Psalm 91

AMERICAN STANDARD VERSION

1 He that dwelleth in the secret place of the Most High shall abide under the shadow of the Almighty.

2 I will say of Jehovah, He is my refuge and my fortress; My God, in whom I trust.

3 For he will deliver thee from the snare of the fowler, and from the deadly pestilence.

4 He will cover thee with his pinions, and under his wings shalt thou take refuge: His truth is a shield and a buckler.

5 Thou shalt not be afraid for the terror by night, nor for the arrow that flieth by day;

6 For the pestilence that walketh in darkness, nor for the destruction that wasteth at noonday.

7 A thousand shall fall at thy side, and ten thousand at thy right hand; (but) it shall not come nigh thee.

8 Only with thine eyes shalt thou behold, and see the reward of the wicked.

9 For thou, O Jehovah, art my refuge! Thou hast made the Most High thy habitation;

10 There shall no evil befall thee, neither shall any plague come nigh thy tent.

11 For he will give his angels charge over thee, to keep thee in all thy ways.

12 They shall bear thee up in their hands, lest thou dash thy foot against a stone.

13 Thou shalt tread upon the lion and adder: the young lion and the serpent shalt thou trample under foot.

14 Because he hath set his love upon me, therefore will I deliver him: I will set him on high, because he hath known my name.

15 He shall call upon me, and I will answer him; I will be with him in trouble: I will deliver him, and honor him.

16 With long life will I satisfy him, and show him my salvation.

NEW AMERICAN STANDARD

1 He who dwells in the shelter of the Most High Will abide in the shadow of the Almighty.

2 I will say to the Lord, "My refuge and my fortress, My God, in whom I trust!"

3 For it is He who delivers you from the snare of the trapper, And from the deadly pestilence.

4 He will cover you with His pinions, And under His wings you may seek refuge; His faithfulness is a shield and bulwark.

5 You will not be afraid of the terror by night, Or of the arrow that flies by day;

6 Of the pestilence that stalks in darkness, Or of the destruction that lays waste at noon.

7 A thousand may fall at your side, And ten thousand at your right hand; But it shall not approach you.

8 You will only look on with your eyes, And see the recompense of the wicked.

9 For you have made the Lord, my refuge, Even the Most High, your dwelling place.

10 No evil will befall you, Nor will any plague come near your tent.

11 For He will give His angels charge concerning you, To guard you in all your ways.

12 They will bear you up in their hands, Lest you strike your foot against a stone.

13 You will tread upon the lion and cobra, The young lion and the serpent you will trample down.

14 Because he has loved Me, therefore I will deliver him; I will set him securely on high, because he has known My name.

15 He will call upon Me, and I will answer him; I will be with him in trouble; I will rescue him, and honor him.

16 With a long life I will satisfy him, And let him behold My salvation.

1 He who dwells in the secret place of the Most High shall remain stable and fixed under the shadow of the Almighty [Whose power no foe can withstand].

2 I will say of the Lord, He is my Refuge and my Fortress, my God; on Him I lean and rely, and in Him I [confidently] trust!

3 For [then] He will deliver you from the snare of the fowler and from the deadly pestilence.

4 [Then] He will cover you with His pinions, and under His wings shall you trust and find refuge; His truth and His faithfulness are a shield and a buckler.

5 You shall not be afraid of the terror of the night, nor of the arrow (the evil plots and slanders of the wicked) that flies by day,

6 Nor of the pestilence that stalks in darkness, nor of the destruction and sudden death that surprise and lay waste at noonday.

7 A thousand may fall at your side, and ten thousand at your right hand, but it shall not come near you.

8 Only a spectator shall you be [yourself inaccessible in the secret place of the Most High] as you witness the reward of the wicked.

9 Because you have made the Lord your refuge, and the Most High your dwelling place, [Ps 91:1,14.]

10 There shall no evil befall you, nor any plague or calamity come near your tent.

11 For He will give His angels [especial] charge over you to accompany and defend and preserve you in all your ways [of obedience and service].

12 They shall bear you up on their hands, lest you dash your foot against a stone. [Luke 4:10,11; Heb 1:14.]

13 You shall tread upon the lion and adder; the young lion and the serpent shall you trample underfoot. [Luke 10:19.]

14 Because he has set his love upon Me, therefore will I deliver him; I will set him on high, because he knows and understands My name [has a personal knowledge of My mercy, love, and kindness-- trusts and relies on Me, knowing I will never forsake him, no, never].

15 He shall call upon Me, and I will answer him; I will be with him in trouble, I will deliver him and honor him.

16 With long life will I satisfy him and show him My salvation.

1   He that dwelleth in the secret place of the Most High shall abide under the shadow of the Almighty.
2   I say of Jehovah, My refuge and my fortress; my God, I will confide in him.
3   Surely he shall deliver thee from the snare of the fowler, [and] from the destructive pestilence.
4   He shall cover thee with his feathers, and under his wings shalt thou find refuge: his truth is a shield and buckler.
5   Thou shalt not be afraid for the terror by night, for the arrow that flieth by day,
6   For the pestilence that walketh in darkness, for the destruction that wasteth at noonday.
7   A thousand shall fall at thy side, and ten thousand at thy right hand; [but] it shall not come nigh thee.
8   Only with thine eyes shalt thou behold, and see the reward of the wicked.
9   Because thou hast made Jehovah, my refuge, the Most High, thy dwelling-place,
10 There shall no evil befall thee, neither shall any plague come nigh thy tent.
11 For he shall give his angels charge concerning thee, to keep thee in all thy ways:
12 They shall bear thee up in [their] hands, lest thou dash thy foot against a stone.
13 Thou shalt tread upon the lion and the adder; the young lion and the dragon shalt thou trample under foot.
14 Because he hath set his love upon me, therefore will I deliver him; I will set him on high, because he hath known my name.
15 He shall call upon me, and I will answer him; I will be with him in trouble, I will deliver him and honour him.
16 With length of days will I satisfy him, and shew him my salvation.

1   He who dwells in the shelter of the Most High will abide in the shadow of the Almighty.

2   I will say to the Lord, "My refuge and my fortress, my God, in whom I trust."

3   For he will deliver you from the snare of the fowler and from the deadly pestilence.

4   He will cover you with his pinions, and under his wings you will find refuge; his faithfulness is a shield and buckler.

5   You will not fear the terror of the night, nor the arrow that flies by day,

6   Nor the pestilence that stalks in darkness, nor the destruction that wastes at noonday.

7   A thousand may fall at your side, ten thousand at your right hand, but it will not come near you.

8   You will only look with your eyes and see the recompense of the wicked.

9   Because you have made the Lord your dwelling place--the Most High, who is my refuge--

10   No evil shall be allowed to befall you, no plague come near your tent.

11   For he will command his angels concerning you to guard you in all your ways.

12   On their hands they will bear you up, lest you strike your foot against a stone.

13   You will tread on the lion and the adder; the young lion and the serpent you will trample underfoot.

14   "Because he holds fast to me in love, I will deliver him; I will protect him, because he knows my name.

15   When he calls to me, I will answer him; I will be with him in trouble; I will rescue him and honor him.

16   With long life I will satisfy him and show him my salvation."

1 Whoever lives under the shelter of the Most High will remain in the shadow of the Almighty.

2 I will say to the Lord, "[You are] my refuge and my fortress, my God in whom I trust."

3 He is the one who will rescue you from hunters' traps and from deadly plagues.

4 He will cover you with his feathers, and under his wings you will find refuge. His truth is your shield and armor.

5 You do not need to fear terrors of the night, arrows that fly during the day,

6 Plagues that roam the dark, epidemics that strike at noon.

7 They will not come near you, even though a thousand may fall dead beside you or ten thousand at your right side.

8 You only have to look with your eyes to see the punishment of wicked people.

9 You, O Lord, are my refuge! You have made the Most High your home.

10 No harm will come to you. No sickness will come near your house.

11 He will put his angels in charge of you to protect you in all your ways.

12 They will carry you in their hands so that you never hit your foot against a rock.

13 You will step on lions and cobras. You will trample young lions and snakes.

14 Because you love me, I will rescue you. I will protect you because you know my name.

15 When you call to me, I will answer you. I will be with you when you are in trouble. I will save you and honor you.

16 I will satisfy you with a long life. I will show you how I will save you.

1 Whoever goes to the Lord for safety, whoever remains under the protection of the Almighty,

2 Can say to him, "You are my defender and protector. You are my God; in you I trust."

3 He will keep you safe from all hidden dangers and from all deadly diseases.

4 He will cover you with his wings; you will be safe in his care; his faithfulness will protect and defend you.

5 You need not fear any dangers at night or sudden attacks during the day

6 Or the plagues that strike in the dark or the evils that kill in daylight.

7 A thousand may fall dead beside you, ten thousand all around you, but you will not be harmed.

8 You will look and see how the wicked are punished.

9 You have made the Lord your defender, the Most High your protector,

10 And so no disaster will strike you, no violence will come near your home.

11 God will put his angels in charge of you to protect you wherever you go.

12 They will hold you up with their hands to keep you from hurting your feet on the stones.

13 You will trample down lions and snakes, fierce lions and poisonous snakes.

14 God says, "I will save those who love me and will protect those who acknowledge me as Lord.

15 When they call to me, I will answer them; when they are in trouble, I will be with them. I will rescue them and honor them.

16 I will reward them with long life; I will save them."

1   The one who lives under the protection of the Most High dwells in the shadow of the Almighty.

2   I will say to the Lord, My refuge and my fortress, my God, in whom I trust.

3   He Himself will deliver you from the hunter's net, from the destructive plague.

4   He will cover you with His feathers; you will take refuge under His wings. His faithfulness will be a protective shield.

5   You will not fear the terror of the night, the arrow that flies by day,

6   The plague that stalks in darkness, or the pestilence that ravages at noon.

7   Though a thousand fall at your side and ten thousand at your right hand, the pestilence will not reach you.

8   You will only see it with your eyes and witness the punishment of the wicked.

9   Because you have made the Lord--my refuge, the most high, your dwelling place,

10 No harm will come to you; no plague will come near your tent.

11 For He will give His angels orders concerning you, to protect you in all your ways.

12 They will support you with their hands so that you will not strike your foot against a stone.

13 You will tread on the lion and the cobra; you will trample the young lion and the serpent.

14 Because he is lovingly devoted to Me, I will deliver him; I will exalt him because he knows My name.

15 When he calls out to Me, I will answer him; I will be with him in trouble. I will rescue him and give him honor.

16 I will satisfy him with a long life and show him My salvation.

1   He that dwelleth in the secret place of the most High shall abide under the shadow of the Almighty.

2   I will say of the Lord, He is my refuge and my fortress: my God; in him will I trust.

3   Surely he shall deliver thee from the snare of the fowler, and from the noisome pestilence.

4   He shall cover thee with his feathers, and under his wings shalt thou trust: his truth shall be thy shield and buckler.

5   Thou shalt not be afraid for the terror by night; nor for the arrow that flieth by day;

6   Nor for the pestilence that walketh in darkness; nor for the destruction that wasteth at noonday.

7   A thousand shall fall at thy side, and ten thousand at thy right hand; but it shall not come nigh thee.

8   Only with thine eyes shalt thou behold and see the reward of the wicked.

9   Because thou hast made the Lord, which is my refuge, even the most High, thy habitation;

10   There shall no evil befall thee, neither shall any plague come nigh thy dwelling.

11   For he shall give his angels charge over thee, to keep thee in all thy ways.

12   They shall bear thee up in their hands, lest thou dash thy foot against a stone.

13   Thou shalt tread upon the lion and adder: the young lion and the dragon shalt thou trample under feet.

14   Because he hath set his love upon me, therefore will I deliver him: I will set him on high, because he hath known my name.

15   He shall call upon me, and I will answer him: I will be with him in trouble; I will deliver him, and honour him.

16   With long life will I satisfy him, and shew him my salvation.

1. He who dwells in the secret place of the Most High Shall abide under the shadow of the Almighty.
2. I will say of the Lord, "He is my refuge and my fortress; My God, in Him I will trust."
3. Surely He shall deliver you from the snare of the fowler And from the perilous pestilence.
4. He shall cover you with His feathers, And under His wings you shall take refuge; His truth shall be your shield and buckler.
5. You shall not be afraid of the terror by night, Nor of the arrow that flies by day,
6. Nor of the pestilence that walks in darkness, Nor of the destruction that lays waste at noonday.
7. A thousand may fall at your side, And ten thousand at your right hand; But it shall not come near you.
8. Only with your eyes shall you look, And see the reward of the wicked.
9. Because you have made the Lord, who is my refuge, Even the Most High, your dwelling place,
10. No evil shall befall you, Nor shall any plague come near your dwelling;
11. For He shall give His angels charge over you, To keep you in all your ways.
12. In their hands they shall bear you up, Lest you dash your foot against a stone.
13. You shall tread upon the lion and the cobra, The young lion and the serpent you shall trample underfoot.
14. "Because he has set his love upon Me, therefore I will deliver him; I will set him on high, because he has known My name.
15. He shall call upon Me, and I will answer him; I will be with him in trouble; I will deliver him and honor him.
16. With long life I will satisfy him, And show him My salvation."

1   Those who go to God Most High for safety will be protected by the Almighty.
2   I will say to the Lord, "You are my place of safety and protection. You are my God and I trust you."
3   God will save you from hidden traps and from deadly diseases.
4   He will cover you with his feathers, and under his wings you can hide. His truth will be your shield and protection.
5   You will not fear any danger by night or an arrow during the day.
6   You will not be afraid of diseases that come in the dark or sickness that strikes at noon.
7   At your side one thousand people may die, or even ten thousand right beside you, but you will not be hurt.
8   You will only watch and see the wicked punished.
9   The Lord is your protection; you have made God Most High your place of safety.
10 Nothing bad will happen to you; no disaster will come to your home.
11 He has put his angels in charge of you to watch over you wherever you go.
12 They will catch you in their hands so that you will not hit your foot on a rock.
13 You will walk on lions and cobras; you will step on strong lions and snakes.
14 The Lord says, "Whoever loves me, I will save. I will protect those who know me.
15 They will call to me, and I will answer them. I will be with them in trouble; I will rescue them and honor them.
16 I will give them a long, full life, and they will see how I can save."

1 He who dwells in the shelter of the Most High will rest in the shadow of the Almighty.

2 I will say of the Lord, "He is my refuge and my fortress, my God, in whom I trust."

3 Surely he will save you from the fowler's snare and from the deadly pestilence.

4 He will cover you with his feathers, and under his wings you will find refuge; his faithfulness will be your shield and rampart.

5 You will not fear the terror of night, nor the arrow that flies by day,

6 Nor the pestilence that stalks in the darkness, nor the plague that destroys at midday.

7 A thousand may fall at your side, ten thousand at your right hand, but it will not come near you.

8 You will only observe with your eyes and see the punishment of the wicked.

9 If you make the Most High your dwelling--even the Lord, who is my refuge--

10 Then no harm will befall you, no disaster will come near your tent.

11 For he will command his angels concerning you to guard you in all your ways;

12 They will lift you up in their hands, so that you will not strike your foot against a stone.

13 You will tread upon the lion and the cobra; you will trample the great lion and the serpent.

14 "Because he loves me," says the Lord, "I will rescue him; I will protect him, for he acknowledges my name.

15 He will call upon me, and I will answer him; I will be with him in trouble, I will deliver him and honor him.

16 With long life will I satisfy him and show him my salvation."

1   The person who rests in the shadow of the Most High God will be kept safe by the Mighty One.

2   I will say about the Lord, "He is my place of safety. He is like a fort to me. He is my God. I trust in him."

3   He will certainly save you from hidden traps and from deadly sickness.

4   He will cover you with his wings. Under the feathers of his wings you will find safety. He is faithful. He will keep you safe like a shield or a tower.

5   You won't have to be afraid of the terrors that come during the night. You won't have to fear the arrows that come at you during the day.

6   You won't have to be afraid of the sickness that attacks in the darkness. You won't have to fear the plague that destroys at noon.

7   A thousand may fall dead at your side. Ten thousand may fall near your right hand. But no harm will come to you.

8   You will see with your own eyes how God punishes sinful people.

9   The Lord is the one who keeps you safe. So let the Most High God be like a home to you.

10 Then no harm will come to you. No terrible plague will come near your tent.

11 The Lord will command his angels to take good care of you.

12 They will lift you up in their hands. Then you won't trip over a stone.

13 You will walk all over lions and cobras. You will crush mighty lions and poisonous snakes.

14 The Lord says, "I will save the one who loves me. I will keep him safe, because he trusts in me.

15 He will call out to me, and I will answer him. I will be with him in times of trouble. I will save him and honor him.

16 I will give him a long and full life. I will save him."

1 Those who live in the shelter of the Most High will find rest in the shadow of the Almighty.

2 This I declare of the Lord: He alone is my refuge, my place of safety; he is my God, and I am trusting him.

3 For he will rescue you from every trap and protect you from the fatal plague.

4 He will shield you with his wings. He will shelter you with his feathers. His faithful promises are your armor and protection.

5 Do not be afraid of the terrors of the night, nor fear the dangers of the day,

6 Nor dread the plague that stalks in darkness, nor the disaster that strikes at midday.

7 Though a thousand fall at your side, though ten thousand are dying around you, these evils will not touch you.

8 But you will see it with your eyes; you will see how the wicked are punished.

9 If you make the Lord your refuge, if you make the Most High your shelter,

10 No evil will conquer you; no plague will come near your dwelling.

11 For he orders his angels to protect you wherever you go.

12 They will hold you with their hands to keep you from striking your foot on a stone.

13 You will trample down lions and poisonous snakes; you will crush fierce lions and serpents under your feet!

14 The Lord says, "I will rescue those who love me. I will protect those who trust in my name.

15 When they call on me, I will answer; I will be with them in trouble. I will rescue them and honor them.

16 I will satisfy them with a long life and give them my salvation."

1   You who sit down in the High God's presence,
     spend the night in Shaddai's shadow,

2   Say this: "God, you're my refuge.
     I trust in you and I'm safe!"

3   That's right--he rescues you from hidden traps,
     shields you from deadly hazards.

4   His huge outstretched arms protect you--
     under them you're perfectly safe;
     his arms fend off all harm.

5   Fear nothing--not wild wolves in the night,
     not flying arrows in the day,

6   Not disease that prowls through the darkness,
     not disaster that erupts at high noon.

7   Even though others succumb all around,
     drop like flies right and left,
     no harm will even graze you.

8   You'll stand untouched, watch it all from a distance,
     watch the wicked turn into corpses.

9   Yes, because God's your refuge,
     the High God your very own home,

10 Evil can't get close to you,
     harm can't get through the door.

11 He ordered his angels
     to guard you wherever you go.

12 If you stumble, they'll catch you;
     their job is to keep you from falling.

13 You'll walk unharmed among lions and snakes,
     and kick young lions and serpents from the path.

14 "If you'll hold on to me for dear life," says God,
     "I'll get you out of any trouble.
     I'll give you the best of care
     if you'll only get to know and trust me.

15 Call me and I'll answer, be at your side in bad times;
     I'll rescue you, then throw you a party.

16 I'll give you a long life,
     give you a long drink of salvation!"

1 He who dwells in the shelter of the Most High, who abides in the shadow of the Almighty,

2 Will say to the Lord, "My refuge and my fortress; my God, in whom I trust."

3 For he will deliver you from the snare of the fowler and from the deadly pestilence;

4 He will cover you with his pinions, and under his wings you will find refuge; his faithfulness is a shield and buckler.

5 You will not fear the terror of the night, nor the arrow that flies by day,

6 Nor the pestilence that stalks in darkness, nor the destruction that wastes at noonday.

7 A thousand may fall at your side, ten thousand at your right hand; but it will not come near you.

8 You will only look with your eyes and see the recompense of the wicked.

9 Because you have made the Lord your refuge, the Most High your habitation,

10 No evil shall befall you, no scourge come near your tent.

11 For he will give his angels charge of you to guard you in all your ways.

12 On their hands they will bear you up, lest you dash your foot against a stone.

13 You will tread on the lion and the adder, the young lion and the serpent you will trample under foot.

14 Because he cleaves to me in love, I will deliver him; I will protect him, because he knows my name.

15 When he calls to me, I will answer him; I will be with him in trouble, I will rescue him and honor him.

16 With long life I will satisfy him, and show him my salvation.

1   You who live in the shelter of the Most High, who abide in the shadow of the Almighty,

2   Will say to the Lord, "My refuge and my fortress; my God, in whom I trust."

3   For he will deliver you from the snare of the fowler and from the deadly pestilence;

4   He will cover you with his pinions, and under his wings you will find refuge; his faithfulness is a shield and buckler.

5   You will not fear the terror of the night, or the arrow that flies by day,

6   Or the pestilence that stalks in darkness, or the destruction that wastes at noonday.

7   A thousand may fall at your side, ten thousand at your right hand, but it will not come near you.

8   You will only look with your eyes and see the punishment of the wicked.

9   Because you have made the Lord your refuge, the Most High your dwelling place,

10   No evil shall befall you, no scourge come near your tent.

11   For he will command his angels concerning you to guard you in all your ways.

12   On their hands they will bear you up, so that you will not dash your foot against a stone.

13   You will tread on the lion and the adder, the young lion and the serpent you will trample under foot.

14   Those who love me, I will deliver; I will protect those who know my name.

15   When they call to me, I will answer them; I will be with them in trouble, I will rescue them and honor them.

16   With long life I will satisfy them, and show them my salvation.

1   He who is dwelling In the secret place of the Most High, In the shade of the Mighty lodgeth habitually,

2   He is saying of Jehovah, "My refuge, and my bulwark, my God, I trust in Him,"

3   For He delivereth thee from the snare of a fowler, From a calamitous pestilence.

4   With His pinion He covereth thee over, And under His wings thou dost trust, A shield and buckler [is] His truth.

5   Thou art not afraid of fear by night, Of arrow that flieth by day,

6   Of pestilence in thick darkness that walketh, Of destruction that destroyeth at noon,

7   There fall at thy side a thousand, And a myriad at thy right hand, Unto thee it cometh not nigh.

8   But with thine eyes thou lookest, And the reward of the wicked thou seest,

9   (For Thou, O Jehovah, [art] my refuge,) The Most High thou madest thy habitation.

10   Evil happeneth not unto thee, And a plague cometh not near thy tent,

11   For His messengers He chargeth for thee, To keep thee in all thy ways,

12   On the hands they bear thee up, Lest thou smite against a stone thy foot.

13   On lion and asp thou treadest, Thou trampest young lion and dragon.

14   Because in Me he hath delighted, I also deliver him--I set him on high, Because he hath known My name.

15   He doth call Me, and I answer him, I [am] with him in distress, I deliver him, and honour him.

16   With length of days I satisfy him, And I cause him to look on My salvation!

1   He who dwells in the secret place of the Most High Will rest in the shadow of the Almighty.

2   I will say of Yahweh, "He is my refuge and my fortress; My God, in whom I trust."

3   For he will deliver you from the snare of the fowler, From the deadly pestilence.

4   He will cover you with his pinions. Under his wings you will take refuge. His truth is a shield and a buckler.

5   You will not be afraid of the terror by night, Nor of the arrow that flies by day;

6   Nor of the pestilence that walks in darkness, Nor of the destruction that wastes at noonday.

7   A thousand may fall at your side, And ten thousand at your right hand; But it will not come near you.

8   You will only look with your eyes, And see the reward of the wicked.

9   For you, Yahweh, are my refuge! You have made the Most High your habitation.

10 No evil shall happen to you, Neither shall any plague come near your dwelling.

11 For he will give his angels charge over you, To guard you in all your ways.

12 They will bear you up in their hands, So that you won't dash your foot against a stone.

13 You will tread on the lion and cobra. You will trample the young lion and the serpent underfoot.

14 "Because he has set his love on me, therefore I will deliver him. I will set him on high, because he has known my name.

15 He will call on me, and I will answer him. I will be with him in trouble. I will deliver him, and honor him.

16 I will satisfy him with long life, And show him my salvation."

1   He that dwelleth in the help of the highest God; shall dwell in the protection of God of heaven. (He who dwelleth in the shelter of the Most High God, shall live under the protection of the God of heaven.)

2   He shall say to the Lord, Thou art mine up-taker, and my refuge; my God, I shall hope in him. (He shall say to the Lord, Thou art my defender, and my refuge; my God, I trust in thee.)

3   For he delivered me from the snare of hunters; and from a sharp word. (For he shall save me from the hunter's snare; and from a sharp word.)

4   With his shoulders he shall make shadow to thee; and thou shalt have hope under his feathers. His truth shall (en)compass thee with a shield; (With his feathers he shall make a shadow for thee; and thou shalt have hope under his wings. His faithfulness shall surround thee like a shield.)

5   Thou shalt not dread of the night's dread. Of an arrow flying in the day, (Thou shalt not fear the terror in the night; nor an arrow flying in the day.)

6   Of a goblin going in darknesses; of assailing, and of a midday fiend. (Nor the pestilence going in darkness; nor the assailing of the plague at midday.)

7   A thousand shall fall down from thy side, and ten thousand from thy right side; forsooth it shall not come nigh to thee. (A thousand shall fall at thy side, and ten thousand at thy right side; but it shall not come even close to thee.)

8   Nevertheless thou shalt behold with thine eyes; and thou shalt see the yielding of sinners. (Nevertheless thou shalt see with thine eyes; yea, thou shalt see the punishment of the sinners.)

9   For thou, Lord, art mine hope; thou hast set thine help (to be the) alder-Highest. (For thou hast made the Lord to be thy hope; yea, the Most High to be thy help.)

10   Evil shall not come to thee; and a scourge shall not (come) nigh to thy tabernacle.

11   For God hath commanded to his angels of thee; that they keep thee in all thy ways. (For God hath commanded his angels to be all around thee; so that they keep thee safe on all thy ways.)

12   They shall bear thee in the hands; lest peradventure thou hurt thy foot at a stone. (They shall lift thee up with their hands; lest thou hurt thy foot on a stone.)

13 Thou shalt go upon a snake, and a cockatrice; and thou shalt defoul a lion, and a dragon (and thou shalt trample upon a lion, and a dragon).

14 (For God saith,) For he hoped in me, I shall deliver him (For God saith, Because he loved me, I shall save him); I shall defend him, for he knew my name.

15 He cried to me, and I shall hear him; I am with him in tribulation; I shall deliver him, and I shall glorify him. (When he crieth to me, I shall answer him; I shall be with him in all his troubles; I shall rescue him, and I shall honour him.)

16 I shall [ful]fill him with the length of days; and I shall show mine health to him. (I shall fulfill him with length of days, that is, with a long life; and I shall give my salvation, or my deliverance, to him/and I shall save him.)

PSALM 91 PERSONALIZED

1 He who dwells in the secret place of the Most High shall abide under Your shadow, Almighty God.

2 I will say of You, Lord, "You are my refuge and my fortress; my God, in You I will trust."

3 Surely You shall deliver me from the snare of the fowler and from the perilous pestilence.

4 You shall cover me with Your feathers, and under Your wings I shall take refuge; Your truth shall be my shield and buckler.

5 I shall not be afraid of the terror by night, nor of the arrow that flies by day,

6 Nor of the pestilence that walks in darkness, nor of the destruction that lays waste at noonday.

7 A thousand may fall at my side, and ten thousand at my right hand; but it shall not come near me.

8 Only with my eyes shall I look, and see the reward of the wicked.

9 Because I have made You Lord, my refuge, even You, oh Most High, my dwelling place,

10 No evil shall befall me, nor shall any plague come near my dwelling;

11 For You shall give Your angels charge over me, to keep me in all my ways.

12 In their hands they shall bear me up, lest I dash my foot against a stone.

13 I shall tread upon the lion and the cobra, the young lion and the serpent I shall trample underfoot.

14 Here is Your promise to me: "Because you have set your love upon Me, therefore I will deliver you; I will set you on high, because you have known My name.

15 You shall call upon Me, and I will answer you; I will be with you in trouble; I will deliver you and honor you.

16 With long life I will satisfy you, and show you My salvation."

I claim these promises today!